BEST-EVER RECIPES
TAPAS & SPANISH

THE AUTHENTIC TASTE OF SPAIN: 130 SUN-DRENCHED CLASSIC DISHES FROM EVERY PART OF SPAIN, SHOWN IN 230 STUNNING PHOTOGRAPHS

Pepita Aris

HERMES HOUSE

This edition is published by Hermes House
an imprint of Anness Publishing Ltd
Hermes House
88–89 Blackfriars Road
London SE1 8HA

www.hermeshouse.com; www.annesspublishing.com

If you like the images in this book and would like to
investigate using them for publishing, promotions or
advertising, please visit our website
www.practicalpictures.com for more information.

Publisher: Joanna Lorenz
Senior Managing Editor: Conor Kilgallon
Photographer: Nicki Dowey
Home Economist: Lucy McKelvie
Assistant Home Economist: Emma McKintosh
Stylist: Helen Trent
Production Controller: Claire Rae

Designed and edited for Anness Publishing Ltd by
the Bridgewater Book Company Ltd

Picture credits: All images copyright Anness Publishing
Ltd except Powerstock 190, 191tl, 191br ©
Purestock/Superstock, 193tl, 193tr, 196; Corbis 192 ©
Robert Wallis, 194 © Jon Hicks, 195 ©Owen Franken,
197 © Peter Adams.

ETHICAL TRADING POLICY
At Anness Publishing we believe that business should be
conducted in an ethical and ecologically sustainable
way, with respect for the environment and a proper
regard to the replacement of the natural resources we
employ.

As a publisher, we use a lot of wood pulp in high-
quality paper for printing, and that wood commonly
comes from spruce trees. We are therefore currently
growing more than 750,000 trees in three Scottish
forest plantations: Berrymoss (130 hectares/320 acres),
West Touxhill (125 hectares/305 acres) and Deveron
Forest (75 hectares/185 acres). The forests we manage
contain more than 3.5 times the number of trees
employed each year in making paper for the books we
manufacture.

Because of this ongoing ecological investment
programme, you, as our customer, can have the pleasure
and reassurance of knowing that a tree is being
cultivated on your behalf to naturally replace the
materials used to make the book you are holding.

Our forestry programme is run in accordance with the
UK Woodland Assurance Scheme (UKWAS) and will be
certified by the internationally recognized Forest
Stewardship Council (FSC). The FSC is a non-
government organization dedicated to promoting
responsible management of the world's forests.
Certification ensures forests are managed in an
environmentally sustainable and socially responsible
way. For further information about this scheme, go to
www.annesspublishing.com/trees

© Anness Publishing Ltd 2007, 2010

A CIP catalogue record for this book is available from
the British Library.

NOTES
For all recipes, quantities are given in both
metric and imperial measures and, where
appropriate, in standard cups and spoons. Follow
one set of measures, but not a mixture, because
they are not interchangeable.

Standard spoon and cup measures are level.
1 tsp = 5ml, 1 tbsp = 15ml, 1 cup = 250ml/8fl
oz. Australian standard tablespoons are 20ml.
Australian readers should use 3 tsp in place of
1 tbsp for measuring small quantities. American
pints are 16fl oz/2 cups. American readers
should use 20fl oz/2.5 cups in place of 1 pint
when measuring liquids.

Electric oven temperatures in this book are
for conventional ovens. When using a fan oven,
the temperature will probably need to be
reduced by about 10–20°C/20–40°F. Since ovens
vary, you should check with your manufacturer's
instruction book for guidance.
The nutritional analysis given for each recipe is
calculated per portion (i.e. serving or item),
unless otherwise stated. If the recipe gives a
range, such as Serves 4–6, then the nutritional
analysis will be for the smaller portion size, i.e. 6
servings. Measurements for sodium do not
include salt added to taste.

Medium (US large) eggs are used unless
otherwise stated.

Front cover shows Seafood Paella – for recipe,
see pages 80–81.

PUBLISHER'S NOTE
Although the advice and information in this book are
believed to be accurate and true at the time of going to
press, neither the authors nor the publisher can accept
any legal responsibility or liability for any errors or
omissions that may have been made nor for any
inaccuracies nor for any loss, harm or injury that comes
about from following instructions or advice in this book.

Contents

Introduction

The history and religion of Spain are visible on the plate. What we eat often says much about who we are and in no country is this more obvious than in Spain. Ingredients, cooking methods and many of Spain's most famous recipes all have an easy-to-trace and fascinating past.

MOORISH INFLUENCES

The Moors invaded Spain from North Africa, in AD711, and stayed for nearly 800 years. The Moorish influence is still evident today. To start with, a huge number of food words are derived from the Arabic: *aceite* (oil), *arroz* (rice), *albóndigas* (meatballs), *almendras* (almonds), *almirez* (the mortar) and *almuerzo* itself, the word for lunch.

From the Moors came new crops, including sugar, spinach, aubergines (eggplants) and mint, and new culinary methods such as cooking in sealed clay pots and the use of wood-burning ovens. The meat skewer and kebabs arrived, and *churrasco* (pieces of meat cooked on the barbecue) is still a Spanish favourite. Frying with olive oil and preserving in vinegar (*escabeche*) were both Arab practices, the latter eagerly adopted by the locals for preserving surplus fish.

The spices brought by the Moors included cinnamon, cumin and nutmeg and the magnificent golden saffron. They enjoyed sour-and-sweet (*agridulce*) mixtures and anise bread. In modern Spain, you will find all these things still on the menu.

CATHOLICISM CONQUERS

The Catholic monarchs Isabella and Ferdinand conquered Granada, the last Moorish stronghold, in 1492. They threw out the Moors and the Jews to make one united Catholic kingdom. The Jews, who had been in Spain for many centuries, left several imprints on Spanish cuisine, including *cocido* (meat and chickpea stew).

The new foods enjoyed in this era were spectacularly different, favoured almost entirely for their religious orthodoxy. *Bacalao* (salt cod) was for Church fast days, of which there were some 200, when abstinence from meat – and sex – was required. Pork, which neither Moors nor Jews would touch, became an integral part of Spanish religion, and therefore everyday life. Eating sausages became a statement of loyalty and proof of conversion to the Catholic church.

FOODS FROM NEW LANDS

The introduction of new foods from America after 1492 changed the Mediterranean diet for ever. Spain was transformed from being a bean, grain and meat-eating country, into a place where vegetables were widely enjoyed. Chocolate and chilli peppers quickly became firm favourites in the Spanish kitchen, tomatoes were adopted and used in sauces, and beans became common.

ABOVE: *The Spanish love to cook and eat outdoors; cooking meat on skewers over a barbecue comes from the Moorish tradition.*

ABOVE: *The slow-cooked stew of meats and chickpeas,* cocido, *was inspired by the Jewish Sabbath stew,* adafina.

ABOVE: *Many classic desserts such as fritters drenched in honey show the Moorish origins of much Spanish food.*

From the opposite direction, the Portuguese, returning from China in the early 1500s, brought with them sweet oranges. The resulting orange trees, which now grow in such abundance all over Spain, have dramatically altered the landscape of the east and south coast.

BETWEEN TWO OCEANS

Spain's longest frontiers are water so it is no wonder the Spanish are seafarers. Spain has always looked outward to the Atlantic as well as inward to the Mediterranean. First came shipping salt, whaling and fishing. Later Cádiz and Sevilla provided the ships and stores for "the Empire on which the sun never sets" – a phrase used to describe the Spanish Empire before it was borrowed by the British.

MEDITERRANEAN LINKS

Since the Phoenicians first arrived and planted olive trees, Spain has long had links with its eastern neighbours. In terms of food influences, Spain has given much more than it has received. The Romans imported Spanish olive oil and adopted Spanish chickpeas to feed their armies. Under the Borgias, Spain introduced beans to Tuscany. When the kings of Aragón ruled Italy, saffron and short-grained rice were planted, which were to become the base of the classic Italian dish, risotto.

You might expect to find French dishes in Spain, but there are actually more Spanish foods to be found in France. France adopted mayonnaise, *aioli*, iced soups, chocolate and tomatoes, plus the beans and spices that transformed their *cassoulet*.

TRAVELLERS AND TOURISM

Spain is a country of mountains, and of fierce regionalism. Nevertheless, it has always had its travellers. The muleteers of León criss-crossed Spain with their load of salt cod and news. They had their own recipe, *bacalao ajo arriero*, which featured dry fish rehydrated in a pot with oil and garlic.

Tourism is not a new trend in Spain. Santiago de Compostela has been a major shrine for pilgrims for a millennium. In the 1550s up to two million people a year walked to Santiago and had to carry their food with them. Nowadays, there are many refuges or restaurants along the route, which provide freshly prepared dishes using local ingredients, such as fresh fish, bread, hams, cheeses, sausages, olives and fruit.

Tapas

In Spain, the motto is "eat when you drink, drink when you eat" – and tapas seem to have been invented for just this. Tapas are finger food, a choice of delicious morsels to tempt the drinker to have another glass and with it another tapas dish. They range from simple dishes of olives and nuts to marinated fish and titbits on skewers.

Sweet and salty vegetable crisps

The Spanish love colourful snacks. Try these brightly coloured vegetable crisps, which make an appealing alternative to the usual potato crisps. Serve them with a bowl of creamy, garlicky aioli, and use the crisps to scoop it up.

SERVES 4

1 small fresh beetroot (beet)
caster (superfine) sugar and fine salt,
**   for sprinkling**
olive oil, for frying
coarse sea salt, to serve

1 Peel the beetroot and, using a mandolin or a vegetable peeler, cut it into very thin slices.

2 Lay the slices on kitchen paper and sprinkle them with sugar and fine salt.

3 Heat 5cm/2in oil in a deep pan until a cube of bread turns golden in 1 minute. Cook the slices in batches, until they float to the surface and turn golden at the edge. Drain on kitchen paper and sprinkle with sea salt once they are cool.

Nutritional information per portion: Energy 155kcal/639kJ; Protein 0.3g; Carbohydrate 1.4g, of which sugars 1.3g; Fat 6.5g, of which saturates 2.4g; Cholesterol 0mg; Calcium 4mg; Fibre 0.4g; Sodium 13mg.

Olive and anchovy bites

These little melt-in-the-mouth morsels are made from two ingredients that are forever associated with tapas – olives and anchovies. The reason for this is that both contain salt, which helps to stimulate thirst and therefore drinking.

MAKES 40–45

115g/4oz/1 cup plain (all-purpose) flour
115g/4oz/¹⁄₂ cup chilled butter, diced
115g/4oz/1 cup finely grated Manchego, mature (sharp) Cheddar or Gruyère cheese
50g/2oz can anchovy fillets in oil, drained and roughly chopped
50g/2oz/¹⁄₂ cup pitted black olives, roughly chopped
2.5ml/¹⁄₂ tsp cayenne pepper
sea salt, to serve (optional)

1 Place the flour, butter, cheese, anchovies, olives and cayenne pepper in a food processor and pulse until the mixture forms a firm dough.

2 Wrap the dough loosely in clear film (plastic wrap). Chill in the refrigerator for 20 minutes.

3 Preheat the oven to 200°C/ 400°F/Gas 6. Remove the dough from the refrigerator, then roll it out thinly on a lightly floured surface.

4 Cut the dough into 5cm/2in wide strips, then cut across each strip in alternate directions, to make triangles. Transfer the triangles to baking sheets and bake for 8–10 minutes until golden. Cool on a wire rack. Sprinkle with sea salt, if desired.

Nutritional information per anchovy bite: Energy 42kcal/173kJ; Protein 1.2g; Carbohydrate 2g, of which sugars 0.1g; Fat 3.2g, of which saturates 1.9g; Cholesterol 9mg; Calcium 27mg; Fibre 0.1g; Sodium 103mg.

Pimiento tartlets

Known as tartalitas de pimiento *in Spain, these pretty little tartlets are filled with strips of roasted sweet peppers and a deliciously creamy custard. They are perfect to serve with drinks.*

SERVES 4

1 red (bell) pepper
1 yellow (bell) pepper
175g/6oz/1½ cups plain (all-purpose) flour
75g/3oz/6 tbsp chilled butter, diced
30–45ml/2–3 tbsp cold water
60ml/4 tbsp double (heavy) cream
1 egg
15ml/1 tbsp freshly grated Parmesan cheese
salt and ground black pepper

1 Preheat the oven to 200°C/400°F/Gas 6, and heat the grill (broiler). Place the peppers on a baking sheet and grill (broil) the peppers for 10 minutes, turning occasionally until blackened. Cover and leave for 5 minutes. Peel off skin, discard the seeds and cut the flesh into strips.

2 Sift the flour and a pinch of salt into a bowl. Rub in the butter until the mixture resembles fine breadcrumbs. Stir in enough water to make a firm, but not sticky, dough.

3 Roll the dough out thinly on a lightly floured surface and line 12 individual moulds or a 12-hole tartlet tin (muffin pan). Prick the bases with a fork and fill the cases with crumpled foil. Bake for 10 minutes. Remove the foil from the pastry cases and divide the pepper strips among the pastry cases.

4 Whisk the cream and egg in a bowl. Season and pour over the peppers. Sprinkle each tartlet with cheese and bake for 15–20 minutes until firm. Cool for 2 minutes, then transfer to a wire rack. Serve the tartlets warm or cold.

Nutritional information per portion: Energy 427kcal/1778kJ; Protein 8.4g; Carbohydrate 40g, of which sugars 6.4g; Fat 27g, of which saturates 16.1g; Cholesterol 112mg; Calcium 131mg; Fibre 2.8g; Sodium 180mg.

Spinach empanadillas

Little pies are part of the Moorish tradition in Spain. The Arabs introduced spinach to Europe and pine nuts and raisins are typical Arab ingredients. In Spain, the dough is sold ready-cut in rounds.

MAKES 20

25g/1oz/¼ cup raisins
25ml/1½ tbsp olive oil
450g/1lb fresh spinach leaves, washed,
   drained and chopped
6 canned anchovies, drained and chopped
2 garlic cloves, finely chopped
25g/1oz/¼ cup pine nuts,
   roughly chopped
350g/12oz puff pastry
1 egg, beaten
salt and ground black pepper

1 To make the filling, soak the raisins in warm water for 10 minutes. Drain well, then chop them roughly.

2 Heat the olive oil in a pan, add the spinach, stir, then cover and cook over a low heat for about 2 minutes until the spinach starts to wilt. Remove the lid, turn up the heat and cook until any liquid has evaporated.

3 Add the anchovies, garlic and seasoning to the spinach and cook, stirring, for 1 minute. Remove from the heat. Stir in the raisins and pine nuts. Cool.

4 Meanwhile, preheat the oven to 180°C/350°F/Gas 4. Roll out the pastry on a lightly floured surface to a 3mm/⅛in thickness.

5 Using a 7.5cm/3in pastry cutter, cut the pastry into 20 rounds. Place about 10ml/2 tsp filling in the middle of each round, then brush the edges with a little water. Bring up the sides of the pastry and seal well. Press the edges together with the back of a fork. Brush with egg.

6 Place the pies on a greased baking sheet and bake for 15 minutes, or until puffed up and golden. Transfer the pies to a wire rack to cool. Serve warm.

Nutritional information per empanadilla: Energy 100kcal/416kJ; Protein 2.4g; Carbohydrate 8.1g, of which sugars 1.8g; Fat 6.8g, of which saturates 0.3g; Cholesterol 10mg; Calcium 62mg; Fibre 0.8g; Sodium 98mg.

Tapas of almonds, olives and cheese

Almonds and olives used to be served free in all tapas bars, and still are in some. They are the perfect nibble for pre-dinner drinks. Manchego cheese in oil is now a delicious Spanish export, although you can easily marinate the cheese yourself.

SERVES 6–8

FOR THE MARINATED OLIVES

2.5ml/¹/₂ tsp coriander seeds
2.5ml/¹/₂ tsp fennel seeds
2 garlic cloves, crushed
5ml/1 tsp chopped fresh rosemary
10ml/2 tsp chopped fresh parsley
15ml/1 tbsp sherry vinegar
30ml/2 tbsp olive oil
115g/4oz/²/₃ cup black olives
115g/4oz/²/₃ cup green olives

FOR THE MARINATED CHEESE
150g/5oz Manchego or other firm cheese
90ml/6 tbsp olive oil

15ml/1 tbsp white wine vinegar
5ml/1 tsp black peppercorns
1 garlic clove, sliced
fresh thyme or tarragon sprigs
fresh flat leaf parsley or tarragon sprigs,
    to garnish (optional)

FOR THE SALTED ALMONDS
1.5ml/¹/₄ tsp cayenne pepper
30ml/2 tbsp sea salt, plus extra for sprinkling
    (optional)
25g/1oz/2 tbsp butter
60ml/4 tbsp olive oil
200g/7oz/1³/₄ cups blanched almonds

1 To make the marinated olives, crush the coriander and fennel seeds in a mortar with a pestle. Work in the garlic, then add the rosemary, parsley, vinegar and olive oil. Put the olives in a small bowl and pour over the marinade. Cover with clear film (plastic wrap) and chill for up to 1 week.

2 To make the marinated cheese, cut the cheese into bitesize pieces, removing any hard rind, and put in a small bowl. Combine the oil, vinegar, peppercorns, garlic and thyme or tarragon and pour over the cheese. Cover with clear film and chill for up to 3 days.

3 To make the salted almonds, combine the cayenne pepper and salt in a bowl. Melt the butter with the oil in a frying pan. Add the almonds and fry them, stirring, for 5 minutes, or until golden. Add the almonds to the salt mixture and toss until the almonds are coated. Leave to cool, then store in an airtight container for up to 1 week.

4 To serve, arrange the almonds, olives and cheese in three separate small, shallow dishes. Garnish the cheese with fresh herbs if you like and sprinkle the almonds with a little more salt, to taste.

Nutritional information per portion: Energy 432kcal/1784kJ; Protein 10.3g; Carbohydrate 1.8g, of which sugars 1.1g; Fat 42.3g, of which saturates 9.7g; Cholesterol 25mg; Calcium 217mg; Fibre 2.7g; Sodium 805mg.

Marinated anchovies

This is one of the simplest ways to prepare these tiny fish because it requires no cooking. Marinating is particularly associated with anchovies, which tend to lose their freshness quickly.

SERVES 4

**225g/8oz fresh anchovies, heads and
    tails removed, and split open along
    the belly**
juice of 3 lemons
30ml/2 tbsp extra virgin olive oil
2 garlic cloves, finely chopped
15ml/1 tbsp chopped fresh parsley
flaked sea salt

1 Place the anchovies on a clean work surface and turn them on to their bellies, then press them down with your thumb.

2 Using the tip of a small, sharp knife, carefully remove the backbones from the flattened fish, and then arrange the anchovies skinside down in a single layer on a large plate.

3 Squeeze two-thirds of the lemon juice over the fish and sprinkle them with the salt. Cover and leave to stand for up to 24 hours, basting occasionally with the juices, until the flesh is white and no longer translucent.

4 Transfer the anchovies to a serving plate and drizzle with the olive oil and the remaining lemon juice. Sprinkle the fish with the chopped garlic and parsley, then cover with clear film (plastic wrap) and chill until ready to serve.

Nutritional information per portion: Energy 144kcal/597kJ; Protein 11.7g; Carbohydrate 0.1g, of which sugars 0.1g; Fat 10.7g, of which saturates 2.3g; Cholesterol 0mg; Calcium 55mg; Fibre 0.2g; Sodium 69mg.

Flash-fried squid with paprika and garlic

This dish can be served as tapas with a fino or manzanilla sherry. Alternatively, serve the squid on a bed of salad leaves, accompanied by bread, for a substantial first course to serve four.

SERVES 6–8

500g/1¼lb very small squid, cleaned
90ml/6 tbsp olive oil
1 fresh red chilli, seeded and
　finely chopped
10ml/2 tsp Spanish mild smoked paprika
30ml/2 tbsp plain (all-purpose) flour
2 garlic cloves, finely chopped
15ml/1 tbsp sherry vinegar
5ml/1 tsp grated lemon rind
30–45ml/2–3 tbsp finely chopped
　fresh parsley
salt and ground black pepper

1 Cut the squid body sacs into rings and cut the tentacles into pieces.

2 Place the squid in a bowl. Mix 30ml/2 tbsp of the olive oil with half the chilli, the paprika, salt and pepper, and pour over the squid. Cover with clear film (plastic wrap), then place in the refrigerator and leave to marinate for 2–4 hours.

3 Toss the squid in the flour and divide it into two batches. Heat the remaining oil in a wok or deep frying pan over a high heat until very hot. Add the first batch of squid and quickly stir-fry for 1–2 minutes, or until it becomes opaque and the tentacles curl.

4 Add half the garlic. Stir, then turn out into a bowl. Repeat with the second batch of squid, adding more oil if needed.

5 Sprinkle with the vinegar, lemon rind, remaining chilli and parsley. Season and serve either hot or cool.

Nutritional information per portion: Energy 139kcal/580kJ; Protein 10.1g; Carbohydrate 3.8g, of which sugars 0.1g; Fat 9.4g, of which saturates 1.4g; Cholesterol 141mg; Calcium 21mg; Fibre 0.3g; Sodium 70mg.

Sizzling prawns

Garlic prawns are hugely popular in Spain, both with and without the addition of chilli. They are normally cooked in small, individual earthenware casseroles, which stand on a traditional thick iron plate – la plancha. A frying pan will produce the same result.

SERVES 4

1–2 dried chillies (to taste)
60ml/4 tbsp olive oil
3 garlic cloves, finely chopped
16 large raw prawns (shrimp), in the shell
French bread, to serve

1 Split the chillies lengthways and discard the seeds. It is best to do this with a knife and fork, because the inner membranes contain a lot of capsaicin, which can be irritating to the eyes, nose and mouth.

2 Heat the oil in a large frying pan and stir-fry the garlic and chilli for 1 minute, until the garlic begins to turn brown.

3 Add the whole prawns and stir-fry for 3–4 minutes, coating them well with the flavoured oil.

4 Remove from the heat and divide the prawns among four dishes. Spoon over the flavoured oil and serve immediately, with French bread. (Remember to provide a plate for the heads and shells, plus plenty of napkins for messy fingers.)

Nutritional information per portion: Energy 147kcal/607kJ; Protein 11g; Carbohydrate 0g, of which sugars 0g; Fat 11.4g, of which saturates 1.6g; Cholesterol 122mg; Calcium 50mg; Fibre 0g; Sodium 119mg.

King prawns in crispy batter

A huge range of prawns are eaten in Spain, each with its appropriate cooking method. Langostinos are deep-water prawns, often with tiger stripes, and can be among the biggest. The best way to enjoy them is dipped in a simple batter and deep-fried.

SERVES 4

120ml/4fl oz/½ cup water
1 large (US extra large) egg
115g/4oz/1 cup plain (all-purpose) flour
5ml/1 tsp cayenne pepper
12 raw king prawns (jumbo shrimp), in the shell
vegetable oil, for deep-frying
flat leaf parsley, to garnish
lemon wedges, to serve (optional)

1 In a large bowl, whisk together the water and the egg. Whisk in the flour and cayenne pepper until the mixture is smooth.

2 Peel the prawns, leaving just the tails intact. Using a sharp knife, make a shallow cut down the back of each prawn.

3 Using the tip of the knife, carefully pull out and discard the dark intestinal tract.

4 Heat the oil in a large pan or deep-fryer, until a cube of bread dropped into the oil browns in 1 minute.

5 Holding the prawns by their tails, dip them into the batter, one at a time, shaking off any excess. Carefully drop each prawn into the oil and fry for 2–3 minutes until crisp and golden. Drain on kitchen paper, garnish with parsley and serve with lemon wedges, if you like.

Nutritional information per portion: Energy 253kcal/1061kJ; Protein 13.1g; Carbohydrate 22.4g, of which sugars 0.4g; Fat 13.1g, of which saturates 1.8g; Cholesterol 145mg; Calcium 87mg; Fibre 0.9g; Sodium 113mg.

Butterflied prawns in chocolate sauce

There is a long tradition in Spain, which originates in Mexico, of cooking savoury food – even shellfish – with chocolate. This dish is known as langostinos en chocolate *in Spanish.*

SERVES 4

8 large raw prawns (shrimp), in the shell
15ml/1 tbsp seasoned plain
  (all-purpose) flour
15ml/1 tbsp pale dry sherry
juice of 1 large orange
15g/¹⁄₂oz dark (bittersweet) chocolate,
  chopped
30ml/2 tbsp olive oil
2 garlic cloves, finely chopped
2.5cm/1in piece fresh root ginger,
  finely chopped
1 small dried chilli, seeded and chopped
salt and ground black pepper

1 Peel the prawns, leaving just the tail sections intact. Make a shallow cut down the back of each one and pull out and discard the dark tract.

2 Turn the prawns over so that the undersides are uppermost, and then cut them open from tail to top, almost to the central back line.

3 Press the prawns down firmly to flatten them. Coat with the flour and set aside. Gently heat the sherry and orange juice in a pan. When warm, remove from the heat and stir in the chopped chocolate until melted.

4 Heat the oil in a large frying pan. Add the chopped garlic, ginger and chilli and cook for 2 minutes until golden. Remove with a slotted spoon and reserve. Add the prawns, cut side down, and cook for 2–3 minutes until golden brown with pink edges. Turn them and cook for a further 2 minutes.

5 Return the garlic mixture to the pan and add the chocolate sauce. Cook for 1 minute, turning the prawns to coat them in the sauce. Season and serve hot.

Nutritional information per portion: Energy 125kcal/520kJ; Protein 8.5g; Carbohydrate 6.5g, of which sugars 3.6g; Fat 6.9g, of which saturates 1.5g; Cholesterol 88mg; Calcium 44mg; Fibre 0.2g; Sodium 88mg.

Spiced clams

Spanish clams, especially in the north, are much larger than clams found elsewhere, and have more succulent bodies. This modern recipe uses Arab spicing to make a hot dip or sauce. Serve with plenty of fresh bread to mop up the delicious juices.

SERVES 3–4

1 small onion, finely chopped
1 celery stick, sliced
2 garlic cloves, finely chopped
2.5cm/1in piece fresh root ginger, grated
30ml/2 tbsp olive oil
1.5ml/¼ tsp chilli powder
5ml/1 tsp ground turmeric
30ml/2 tbsp chopped fresh parsley
500g/1¼lb small clams, in the shell
30ml/2 tbsp dry white wine
salt and ground black pepper
celery leaves, to garnish
fresh bread, to serve

1 Place the onion, celery, garlic and ginger in a large pan, add the olive oil, spices and chopped parsley and stir-fry for about 5 minutes. Add the clams to the pan and cook for 2 minutes.

2 Add the wine, then cover and cook gently for 2–3 minutes, shaking the pan occasionally. Season. Discard any clams whose shells remain closed, then serve, garnished with the celery leaves.

COOK'S TIP

There are many varieties of clam. The almeja fina *(carpet shell clam) is perfect for this dish. Before cooking, check that all the shells are closed, and discard any that do not close when tapped. Discard any clams that do not open after cooking.*

Nutritional information per portion: Energy 92kcal/381kJ; Protein 6.5g; Carbohydrate 2.2g, of which sugars 1.1g; Fat 5.9g, of which saturates 0.9g; Cholesterol 25mg; Calcium 50mg; Fibre 0.7g; Sodium 458mg.

Mussels with a parsley crust

The stormy Atlantic coast of Spain produces the best mussels in the world. They grow to an enormous size very quickly, without becoming tough. Here they are grilled with a delicious topping, which helps to stop them becoming overcooked.

SERVES 4

450g/1lb fresh mussels
45ml/3 tbsp water
15ml/1 tbsp melted butter
15ml/1 tbsp olive oil
45ml/3 tbsp freshly grated
   Parmesan cheese

30ml/2 tbsp chopped fresh parsley
2 garlic cloves, finely chopped
2.5ml/$^1/_2$ tsp coarsely ground
   black pepper
crusty bread, to serve

1 Scrub the mussels thoroughly, scraping off any barnacles with a round-bladed knife and pulling out the gritty beards. Sharply tap any open mussels and discard any that fail to close or whose shells are broken.

2 Place the mussels in a large pan and add the water. Cover the pan with a lid and steam for about 5 minutes, or until the mussel shells have opened.

3 Drain the mussels well and discard any that remain closed. Carefully snap off the top shell from each mussel, leaving the actual flesh still attached to the bottom shell.

4 Balance the shells upright in a flameproof dish, packing them closely together to make sure that they stay level.

5 Preheat the grill (broiler) to high. Put the melted butter, olive oil, Parmesan cheese, parsley, garlic and black pepper in a small bowl and mix well to combine.

6 Spoon a small amount of the cheese and garlic mixture on top of each mussel and gently press down with the back of the spoon.

7 Grill (broil) the mussels for about 2 minutes, or until they are sizzling and golden. Serve the mussels in their shells, with bread to mop up the juices.

Nutritional information per portion: Energy 110kcal/456kJ; Protein 5.4g; Carbohydrate 0.3g, of which sugars 0.3g; Fat 9.7g, of which saturates 4.7g; Cholesterol 21mg; Calcium 165mg; Fibre 0.6g; Sodium 156mg.

Chicken croquettes

Croquetas are popular tapas fare and there are many variations. This one is based on béchamel sauce, which is perfect for taking on different flavours such as ham or chopped peppers.

SERVES 4

25g/1oz/2 tbsp butter
25g/1oz/¼ cup plain (all-purpose) flour
150ml/¼ pint/²/₃ cup milk
15ml/1 tbsp olive oil, plus extra for
   deep-frying
1 boneless chicken breast with skin, diced
1 garlic clove, finely chopped
1 small egg, beaten
50g/2oz/1 cup stale white breadcrumbs
salt and ground black pepper
fresh flat leaf parsley, to garnish
lemon wedges, to serve

1 Melt the butter in a pan. Add the flour and cook gently, stirring, for 1 minute. Gradually stir in the milk and cook until smooth and thick. Cover and set aside.

2 Heat the oil in a frying pan and fry the diced chicken and garlic together, turning, for 5 minutes.

3 When the chicken is lightly browned and cooked through, put the contents of the frying pan into a food processor and process until finely chopped. Add the mixture to the sauce and stir to combine. Season to taste, then leave to cool.

4 Once cooled and firm, shape the mixture into eight small sausage shapes. Dip each one in beaten egg, then roll in breadcrumbs to coat.

5 Heat the oil in a pan, until a cube of bread dropped in the oil browns in 1 minute. Lower the croquettes into the oil and cook for 4 minutes until crisp and golden, then drain on kitchen paper. Serve with lemon wedges and garnish with parsley.

Nutritional information per portion: Energy 286kcal/1195kJ; Protein 13.9g; Carbohydrate 16.4g, of which sugars 2.2g; Fat 18.9g, of which saturates 5.8g; Cholesterol 89mg; Calcium 80mg; Fibre 0.5g; Sodium 189mg.

Barbecued mini ribs

These tasty ribs are known as costillas *in Spain. They are delicious cooked on a barbecue or under a hot grill. If you prefer a sweeter flavour, use freshly squeezed orange juice instead of sherry.*

SERVES 6–8

1 sheet of pork ribs, about 675g/1¹/₂lb
90ml/6 tbsp sweet oloroso sherry
15ml/1 tbsp tomato purée (paste)
5ml/1 tsp soy sauce
2.5ml/¹/₂ tsp Tabasco sauce
**15ml/1 tbsp light muscovado
    (brown) sugar**
**30ml/2 tbsp seasoned plain
    (all-purpose) flour**
coarse sea salt

1 Separate the ribs, then, using a meat cleaver or heavy knife, cut each rib in half widthways to make about 30 pieces.

2 Mix the sherry, tomato purée, soy sauce, Tabasco and sugar together in a bowl. Stir in 2.5ml/¹/₂ tsp salt.

3 Put the seasoned flour in a strong plastic bag, then add the ribs and toss to coat. Dip each rib in the sauce. Cook on a hot barbecue or under a hot grill (broiler) for 30–40 minutes, turning occasionally until cooked and a little charred. Sprinkle with salt and serve.

COOK'S TIP
Oloroso sherry has a full body and sweet flavour sometimes reminiscent of port.

Nutritional information per portion: Energy 469kcal/1977kJ; Protein 15g; Carbohydrate 66.7g, of which sugars 3.9g; Fat 16.8g, of which saturates 5.5g; Cholesterol 38mg; Calcium 193mg; Fibre 2.7g; Sodium 1146mg.

Buñuelos

The name of these cheese puffs literally means puffball. In Spain, they are usually deep-fried, but baking is easier and gives wonderful results. The dough is made in the same way as French choux pastry, and the buñuelos should be eaten within a few hours of baking.

SERVES 4

50g/2oz/¼ cup butter, diced
1.5ml/¼ tsp salt
250ml/8fl oz/1 cup water
115g/4oz/1 cup plain (all-purpose) flour
2 whole eggs, plus 1 yolk
2.5ml/½ tsp Dijon mustard
2.5ml/½ tsp cayenne pepper
50g/2oz/½ cup finely grated Manchego or Cheddar cheese

1 Preheat the oven to 220°C/425°F/Gas 7. Place the butter and the salt in a pan, then add the water. Bring the liquid to the boil. Meanwhile, sift the flour on to a sheet of baking parchment or greaseproof (waxed) paper.

2 Working quickly, tip the flour into the pan of boiling liquid in one go and stir it in immediately. Beat the mixture vigorously with a wooden spoon until it forms a thick paste that binds together and leaves the sides of the pan clean. Remove the pan from the heat.

3 Gradually beat the eggs and yolk into the mixture, then add the mustard, cayenne pepper and cheese.

4 Place teaspoonfuls of mixture on a non-stick baking sheet and bake for 10 minutes. Reduce the temperature to 180°C/350°F/Gas 4. Cook for 15 minutes until well browned. Serve hot or cold.

Nutritional information per portion: Energy 296kcal/1235kJ; Protein 9.9g; Carbohydrate 22.5g, of which sugars 0.6g; Fat 18.9g, of which saturates 10.5g; Cholesterol 184mg; Calcium 156mg; Fibre 0.9g; Sodium 223mg.

Chicharrones

The Spanish eat everything that comes from the pig, and even the humble rind goes into making this delicious little salted, piquant snack. This crispy, crunchy pork crackling is the perfect accompaniment for a glass of wine or chilled bottle of lager.

SERVES 4

115g/4oz pork rind
vegetable oil, for frying
paprika and coarse sea salt, for sprinkling

1 Using a sharp knife, cut the pork rind into strips. There is no need to be too precise, but try to make the strips roughly 1cm/½in wide and 2.5cm/1in long.

2 Pour the vegetable oil to a depth of 2.5cm/1in in a deep, heavy frying pan. Heat the oil and check that it has reached the correct temperature by immersing a cube of bread, which should brown in 1 minute.

3 Cook the strips of rind in the oil for 1–2 minutes, until they are puffed up and golden brown. Remove with a slotted spoon and drain on kitchen paper.

4 Sprinkle the chicharrones with paprika and salt to taste. Serve them hot or cold. Although they are at their best 1–2 days after cooking, they will keep reasonably well for up to 2 weeks in an airtight container.

Nutritional information per portion: Energy 247kcal/1018kJ; Protein 4.1g; Carbohydrate 0g, of which sugars 0g; Fat 25g, of which saturates 6.4g; Cholesterol 28mg; Calcium 3mg; Fibre 0g; Sodium 20mg.

Pinchitos moruños

The Moors introduced both skewers and marinated meat to Spain. These little yellow kebabs are a favourite in Andalusia, where many butchers sell the meat ready marinated. The Arab versions used lamb, but pork is used now, because the spicing fits so perfectly.

SERVES 4

2.5ml/¹/₂ tsp cumin seeds
2.5ml/¹/₂ tsp coriander seeds
2 garlic cloves, finely chopped
5ml/1 tsp paprika
2.5ml/¹/₂ tsp dried oregano

15ml/1 tbsp lemon juice
45ml/3 tbsp olive oil
500g/1¹/₄lb lean cubed pork
salt and ground black pepper

1 Starting a couple of hours in advance, grind the cumin and coriander seeds in a mortar and work in the garlic with a pinch of salt. Add the paprika and oregano and mix in the lemon juice. Stir in the oil.

2 Cut the pork into small cubes, then skewer them, three or four at a time, on to cocktail sticks (toothpicks). Put the skewered meat in a shallow dish, and pour over the marinade. Spoon the marinade back over the meat to ensure that it is well coated. Leave to marinate in a cool place for 2 hours.

3 Preheat the grill (broiler) to high, and line the grill pan with foil. Spread the kebabs out in a row and place under the grill, close to the heat. Cook for about 3 minutes on each side, spooning the juices over when you turn them, until cooked through. Sprinkle with salt and pepper, and serve.

Nutritional information per portion: Energy 233kcal/970kJ; Protein 27g; Carbohydrate 0.7g, of which sugars 0g; Fat 13.5g, of which saturates 2.9g; Cholesterol 79mg; Calcium 25mg; Fibre 0.6g; Sodium 99mg.

Soups and eggs

Gazpacho is a world-famous soup, but there are many other delicious recipes, from light dishes to hearty soups that are meals in themselves. Tortilla is the quintessential Spanish dish, and eggs hold a special place in the Spanish heart – for they symbolize the countryside, where many dream of setting up home.

Gazpacho

This classic chilled soup is deeply rooted in Andalusia. The flavoursome blend of tomatoes, sweet peppers and garlic is sharpened with sherry vinegar, and enriched with olive oil. Serving it with saucerfuls of garnishes has virtually become a tradition.

SERVES 4

1.3–1.6kg/3–3¹/₂lb ripe tomatoes
1 green (bell) pepper, seeded and
    roughly chopped
2 garlic cloves, finely chopped
2 slices stale bread, crusts removed
60ml/4 tbsp extra virgin olive oil
60ml/4 tbsp sherry vinegar
150ml/¹/₄ pint/²/₃ cup tomato juice
300ml/¹/₂ pint/1¹/₄ cups iced water
salt and ground black pepper
ice cubes, to serve (optional)

FOR THE GARNISHES

30ml/2 tbsp olive oil
2–3 slices stale bread, diced
1 small cucumber, peeled and finely diced
1 small onion, finely chopped
1 red and 1 green (bell) pepper,
    seeded and finely diced
2 hard-boiled eggs, chopped

1 Skin the tomatoes, then quarter them and remove the cores and seeds, saving the juices. Put the pepper in a food processor and process for a few seconds. Add the tomatoes, reserved juices, garlic, bread, oil and vinegar and process. Add the tomato juice and blend until it is combined.

2 Season the soup, then pour into a large bowl, cover with clear film (plastic wrap) and chill for at least 12 hours.

3 Prepare the garnishes. Heat the olive oil in a frying pan and fry the bread cubes for 4–5 minutes until golden brown and crisp. Drain well on kitchen paper, then arrange in a small dish. Place the remaining garnishes in separate small dishes.

4 Just before serving, dilute the soup with the ice-cold water. The consistency should be thick but not stodgy. If you like, stir a few ice cubes into the soup, then serve with the garnishes.

Nutritional information per portion: Energy 376kcal/1584kJ; Protein 11.3g; Carbohydrate 38.3g, of which sugars 31.3g; Fat 21.1g, of which saturates 3.6g; Cholesterol 95mg; Calcium 109mg; Fibre 8.3g; Sodium 103mg.

Chilled almond soup with grapes

Called ajo blanco *– white garlic soup – in Spain, this is a chilled Moorish soup of ancient origin. It is a perfect balance of three southern ingredients: crushed almonds, garlic and vinegar, in a smooth purée made luscious with oil.*

SERVES 6

115g/4oz stale white bread
115g/4oz/1 cup blanched almonds
2 garlic cloves, sliced
75ml/5 tbsp olive oil
25ml/1¹/₂ tbsp sherry vinegar
salt and ground black pepper

FOR THE GARNISH
toasted flaked (sliced) almonds
green and black grapes, halved
  and seeded
chopped fresh chives

1 Break the bread into a bowl and pour in 150ml/¹/₄ pint/²/₃ cup cold water. Leave to soak for about 5 minutes, then squeeze dry.

2 Put the almonds and garlic in a food processor or blender and process until very finely ground. Add the soaked white bread and process again until thoroughly combined.

3 Continue to process, gradually adding the oil until the mixture forms a smooth paste. Add the

sherry vinegar, followed by 600ml/ 1 pint/2¹/₂ cups cold water and process until the mixture is smooth.

4 Transfer the soup to a bowl and season with plenty of salt and pepper, adding a little more water if the soup is very thick. Cover with clear film (plastic wrap) and chill for at least 2 hours.

5 Ladle the soup into bowls. Sprinkle the almonds, halved grapes and chopped chives over to garnish.

Nutritional information per portion: Energy 246kcal/1023kJ; Protein 5.8g; Carbohydrate 11.1g, of which sugars 1.3g; Fat 20.2g, of which saturates 2.2g; Cholesterol 0mg; Calcium 67mg; Fibre 1.8g; Sodium 103mg.

Catalan broad bean and potato soup

Habas are fresh broad beans, and are much nicer than the dried variety, known as favas. The word has vanished from the Spanish dictionary and the dried bean has all but disappeared as well. This soup also uses an uncommon herb in Spanish cooking – coriander – but it adds a delicious flavour.

SERVES 4

30ml/2 tbsp olive oil

2 onions, chopped

3 large floury potatoes, peeled and diced

450g/1lb fresh shelled broad (US fava)
   beans, plus extra to garnish

1.75 litres/3 pints/7¹/₂ cups
   vegetable stock

1 bunch fresh coriander (cilantro),
   roughly chopped

150ml/¹/₄ pint/²/₃ cup single (light)
   cream, plus a little extra to garnish

salt and ground black pepper

1 Heat the oil in a large pan and fry the onions, stirring, for 5 minutes until soft. Add the potatoes, most of the beans (reserving a few for the garnish) and the stock, and bring to the boil. Simmer for 5 minutes, then add the coriander and simmer for a further 10 minutes.

2 Blend the soup in batches in a food processor or blender, then return to the rinsed pan.

3 Stir in the cream, season to taste, and bring to a simmer. Serve garnished with beans, cream and coriander sprigs.

Nutritional information per portion: Energy 358kcal/1504kJ; Protein 14.3g; Carbohydrate 46.4g, of which sugars 10.1g; Fat 14.2g, of which saturates 5.6g; Cholesterol 21mg; Calcium 156mg; Fibre 10.9g; Sodium 44mg.

Chilled avocado soup with cumin

Andalusia is home to both avocados and gazpacho, so it is not surprising that this chilled avocado soup, which is also known as green gazpacho, was invented there. In Spain, this deliciously mild, creamy soup is known as sopa de aguacate.

SERVES 4

3 ripe avocados
1 bunch spring onions (scallions),
    white parts only, trimmed and
    roughly chopped
2 garlic cloves, chopped
juice of 1 lemon
1.5ml/¼ tsp ground cumin
1.5ml/¼ tsp paprika
450ml/¾ pint/scant 2 cups fresh chicken
    stock, cooled, and all fat skimmed off
300ml/½ pint/1¼ cups iced water
salt and ground black pepper
chopped fresh flat leaf parsley, to serve

1 Starting half a day ahead, put the flesh of one avocado in a food processor or blender. Add the spring onions, garlic and lemon juice and purée until smooth. Add the second avocado and purée, then the third, with the spices and seasoning. Purée until smooth.

2 Gradually add the stock. Pour the soup into a bowl and chill it for several hours.

3 To serve, stir in the iced water, then season to taste with plenty of salt and black pepper. Garnish with chopped parsley and then serve.

Nutritional information per portion: Energy 151kcal/623kJ; Protein 2.1g; Carbohydrate 2.6g, of which sugars 1.1g; Fat 14.6g, of which saturates 3.1g; Cholesterol 0mg; Calcium 19mg; Fibre 3g; Sodium 6mg.

Sopa de mariscos

This Mediterranean seafood soup can be served as a main course for four or it can be diluted with white wine and water to make an appetizer for six.

SERVES 4

675g/1¹/₂lb raw prawns (shrimp), in the shell

900ml/1¹/₂ pints/3³/₄ cups cold water

1 onion, chopped

1 celery stick, chopped

1 bay leaf

45ml/3 tbsp olive oil

2 slices stale bread, crusts removed

1 small onion, finely chopped

1 large garlic clove, chopped

2 large tomatoes, halved

¹/₂ large green (bell) pepper, finely chopped

500g/1¹/₄lb cockles (small clams) or mussels, cleaned

juice of 1 lemon

45ml/3 tbsp chopped fresh parsley

5ml/1 tsp paprika

salt and ground black pepper

1 Pull the heads off the prawns and put them in a pan with the cold water. Add the onion, celery and bay leaf and simmer for 20–25 minutes. Peel the prawns, adding the shells to the stock.

2 Heat the oil in a large pan and fry the bread slices quickly, then reserve them. Fry the onion until it is soft, adding the garlic towards the end.

3 Scoop the seeds out of the tomatoes and discard. Chop the flesh and add to the pan with the green pepper. Fry briefly, stirring occasionally. Strain the stock into the pan and bring to the boil. Check over the cockles or mussels, discarding any that are open or damaged.

4 Add half the cockles or mussels to the stock. When open, transfer some of them out on to a plate. Remove the mussels or cockles from the shells and discard the shells. (You should end up having discarded about half of the shells.) Meanwhile, repeat the process to cook the remaining cockles or mussels.

5 Return the cockles or mussels to the soup and add the prawns. Add the bread, torn into little pieces, and the lemon juice and chopped parsley. Season to taste with paprika, salt and pepper and stir gently to mix in the bread. Serve.

Nutritional information per portion: Energy 301kcal/1266kJ; Protein 39.5g; Carbohydrate 13.5g, of which sugars 6.3g; Fat 10.3g, of which saturates 1.6g; Cholesterol 362mg; Calcium 223mg; Fibre 1.9g; Sodium 709mg.

Sherried onion soup with saffron

The Spanish combination of onions, sherry and saffron gives this pale yellow soup a beguiling taste that is perfect for the opening course of a meal. The addition of ground almonds to thicken the soup gives it a wonderful texture and flavour.

SERVES 4

40g/1¹/₂oz/3 tbsp butter
2 large yellow onions, thinly sliced
1 small garlic clove, finely chopped
pinch of saffron threads (0.25g)
50g/2oz blanched almonds, toasted and
    finely ground
750ml/1¹/₄ pints/3 cups chicken or
    vegetable stock
45ml/3 tbsp fino sherry
2.5ml/¹/₂ tsp paprika
salt and ground black pepper

FOR THE GARNISH

30ml/2 tbsp flaked or sliced almonds,
    toasted
chopped fresh parsley

1 Melt the butter in a heavy pan over a low heat. Add the onions and garlic, stirring to ensure that they are thoroughly coated in the melted butter, then cover the pan and cook very gently, stirring frequently, for about 20 minutes, or until the onions are soft and golden yellow.

2 Add the saffron threads to the pan and cook, uncovered, for 3–4 minutes, then add the finely ground almonds and cook, stirring the ingredients constantly, for a further 2–3 minutes. Pour the chicken or vegetable stock and sherry into the pan and stir in 5ml/1 tsp salt and the paprika. Season with plenty of black pepper. Bring to the boil, then lower the heat and simmer gently for about 10 minutes.

3 Pour the soup into a food processor and process until smooth, then return it to the rinsed pan. Reheat slowly, without allowing the soup to boil, stirring occasionally. Taste for seasoning, adding more salt and pepper if required. Ladle the soup into heated bowls, garnish with the toasted flaked or sliced almonds and a little chopped fresh parsley and serve immediately.

Nutritional information per portion: Energy 246kcal/1017kJ; Protein 5.5g; Carbohydrate 9.5g, of which sugars 6.7g; Fat 19.6g, of which saturates 6.1g; Cholesterol 21mg; Calcium 76mg; Fibre 2.9g; Sodium 68mg.

Sopa Castiliana

This rich, dark garlic soup, which comes from La Mancha, a poor region in central Spain, has harsh, strong tastes to match the hot, dry climate. People either love it or hate it. Poaching a whole egg in each bowl just before serving transforms the soup into a meal.

SERVES 4

30ml/2 tbsp olive oil
4 large garlic cloves, peeled
4 slices stale country bread
20ml/4 tsp paprika
1 litre/1¾ pints/4 cups beef stock
1.5ml/¼ tsp ground cumin
4 eggs
salt and ground black pepper
chopped fresh parsley, to garnish

1 Preheat the oven to 230°C/450°F/Gas 8. Heat the olive oil in a large pan. Add the whole peeled garlic cloves and cook gently until they are golden, then remove and set aside. Fry the slices of bread in the oil until they are golden, then set these aside.

2 Add 15ml/1 tbsp of the paprika to the pan, and fry for a few seconds. Stir in the beef stock, cumin and remaining paprika, then add the reserved garlic, crushing the cloves with the back of a wooden spoon. Season to taste, then cook for about 5 minutes.

3 Break up the slices of fried bread into bitesize pieces and stir them into the soup. Ladle the soup into four ovenproof bowls. Carefully break an egg into each bowl of soup and place in the oven for about 3 minutes, until the eggs are set. Sprinkle the soup with chopped fresh parsley and serve immediately.

Nutritional information per portion: Energy 208kcal/870kJ; Protein 9.5g; Carbohydrate 16.5g, of which sugars 0.8g; Fat 12.3g, of which saturates 2.4g; Cholesterol 190mg; Calcium 71mg; Fibre 0.5g; Sodium 228mg.

Fish soup with orange

The old name for this soup is sopa cachorreña – *Seville orange soup – and it is good served post-Christmas, when Seville oranges are in season. It has a beautiful orange colour. The fish used is normally small hake, but any white fish is suitable.*

SERVES 6

1kg/2¼lb small hake or whiting, whole
   but cleaned
1.2 litres/2 pints/5 cups water
4 bitter oranges or 4 sweet oranges and
   2 lemons
30ml/2 tbsp olive oil
5 garlic cloves, unpeeled

1 large onion, finely chopped
1 tomato, peeled, seeded and chopped
4 small potatoes, cut into rounds
5ml/1 tsp paprika
salt and ground black pepper
15–30ml/1–2 tbsp finely chopped fresh
   parsley, to garnish

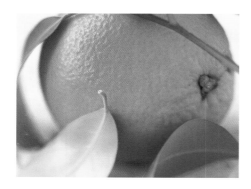

1 Fillet the fish and cut each fillet into three, reserving all the trimmings. Put the fillets on a plate, salt lightly and chill. Put the trimmings in a pan, add the water and a spiral of orange rind. Bring to a simmer, skim, then cover and cook gently for 30 minutes.

2 Heat the oil in a large pan over a high heat. Smash the garlic cloves with the flat of a knife and fry until they are well coloured. Discard them and turn down the heat. Fry the onion gently until it is softened, adding the tomato halfway through.

3 Strain in the hot fish stock (adding the orange spiral as well if you wish) and bring back to the boil. Add the potatoes to the pan and cook them for about 5 minutes.

4 Add the fish pieces to the soup, a few at a time, without letting it go off the boil. Cook for about 15 minutes. Add the squeezed orange juice and lemon juice, if using, and the paprika, with salt and pepper to taste. Serve in bowls, garnished with a little parsley.

Nutritional information per portion: Energy 223kcal/937kJ; Protein 18.3g; Carbohydrate 25.2g, of which sugars 11.7g; Fat 6.1g, of which saturates 0.9g; Cholesterol 19mg; Calcium 86mg; Fibre 3.5g; Sodium 103mg.

Spicy sausage and cheese tortilla

This substantial tortilla is delicious hot or cold. Cut it into wedges and serve for supper with a tomato and basil salad. Adding spicy chorizo and tangy cheese gives it a wonderful, rich flavour.

SERVES 4–6

75ml/5 tbsp olive oil

175g/6oz frying chorizo or spicy sausage, thinly sliced

675g/1¹/₂lb waxy potatoes, thinly sliced

2 Spanish onions, halved and thinly sliced

4 large (US extra large) eggs

30ml/2 tbsp chopped fresh parsley, plus extra to garnish

115g/4oz/1 cup grated Cheddar or other hard cheese

salt and ground black pepper

1 Heat 15ml/1 tbsp of the oil in a 23cm/9in frying pan and fry the sausage until golden and cooked through. Drain on kitchen paper.

2 Add a further 30ml/2 tbsp oil to the pan and fry the potatoes and onions for 2–3 minutes, turning frequently. Cover tightly and cook over a gentle heat for about 30 minutes, turning occasionally, until softened and slightly golden.

3 In a large mixing bowl, beat together the eggs, parsley, cheese, sausage and plenty of seasoning. Gently stir in the potatoes and onions until coated.

4 Wipe out the pan with kitchen paper and heat the remaining 30ml/2 tbsp oil. Add the potato mixture and cook, over a very low heat, until the egg begins to set. Use a metal spatula to prevent the tortilla sticking and to allow the uncooked egg to run underneath.

5 Preheat the grill (broiler) to high. When the base of the tortilla has set, which should take about 5 minutes, protect the pan handle with foil and place the tortilla under the grill until it is set and golden. Cut into wedges and serve garnished with parsley.

Nutritional information per portion: Energy 409kcal/1703kJ; Protein 14.9g; Carbohydrate 28.3g, of which sugars 6.8g; Fat 26.7g, of which saturates 9.5g; Cholesterol 157mg; Calcium 212mg; Fibre 2.7g; Sodium 438mg.

Tortilla with beans

The addition of chopped herbs and skinned beans to the classic tortilla makes this a very summery dish. Enjoy it for lunch, or cut it into small pieces and serve as tapas.

SERVES 2

45ml/3 tbsp olive oil
2 Spanish onions, thinly sliced
300g/11oz waxy potatoes, cut into dice
**250g/9oz/1¾ cups shelled broad
    (fava) beans**
**5ml/1 tsp chopped fresh thyme or
    summer savory**
6 large (US extra large) eggs
**45ml/3 tbsp mixed chopped fresh chives
    and fresh flat leaf parsley**
salt and ground black pepper

1 Heat 30ml/2 tbsp of the oil in a 23cm/9in deep non-stick frying pan. Add the onions and potatoes and stir to coat. Cover and cook gently, stirring, for 20–25 minutes until the potatoes are cooked.

2 Meanwhile, cook the beans in a pan of boiling salted water for 5 minutes. Drain and set aside to cool.

3 When the beans are cool enough to handle, peel off and discard the grey outer skins. Add the beans to the frying pan, together with the thyme or summer savory, and season to taste. Stir well to mix and cook for a further 2–3 minutes.

4 Beat the eggs with salt and pepper to taste and add the mixed herbs, then pour over the potatoes and onions and increase the heat. Cook gently for 5 minutes, or until the bottom browns. During cooking, pull the tortilla away from the sides of the pan and tilt it to allow the uncooked egg to run underneath.

5 Cover the pan with a plate and invert the tortilla on to it. Add the remaining oil to the pan and heat. Slip the tortilla back into the pan, uncooked side down, and cook for 3–5 minutes until the underneath turns brown. Slide the tortilla out on to a plate. Cut it up and serve warm.

Nutritional information per portion: Energy 637kcal/2662kJ; Protein 33.7g; Carbohydrate 51.3g, of which sugars 12.5g; Fat 35g, of which saturates 7.3g; Cholesterol 571mg; Calcium 247mg; Fibre 12.9g; Sodium 249mg.

Potato tortilla

The classic tortilla stands on every tapas bar in Spain. The size of a large cake, it is very satisfying. It can be eaten in wedges – a meal in itself with salad – or cut into chunks and enjoyed as a snack.

SERVES 6

450g/1lb small waxy potatoes, peeled
1 Spanish onion
45ml/3 tbsp vegetable oil
4 large (US extra large) eggs
salt and ground black pepper
fresh flat leaf parsley or tomato wedges,
    to garnish

1 Using a sharp knife, cut the potatoes into thin slices and slice the onion into thin rings. Heat 30ml/2 tbsp of the oil in a 20cm/8in heavy frying pan.

2 Add the potatoes and the onions to the pan and cook over a low heat for 20 minutes, or until the potato slices are just tender. Remove from the heat.

3 In a large bowl, beat together the eggs with a little salt and pepper. Stir in the potatoes and onion.

4 Clean the frying pan with kitchen paper then heat the remaining oil and pour in the potato mixture. Cook very gently for 5–8 minutes until set underneath. During cooking, lift the edges of the tortilla with a spatula, and allow any uncooked egg to run underneath. Shake the pan from side to side, to prevent sticking.

5 Place a large heatproof plate upside-down over the pan, invert the tortilla on to the plate and then slide it back into the pan. Cook for 2–3 minutes more, until the underside of the tortilla is golden brown. Cut into wedges and serve, garnished with fresh flat leaf parsley or tomato wedges.

Nutritional information per portion: Energy 163kcal/681kJ; Protein 5.8g; Carbohydrate 14.7g, of which sugars 2.8g; Fat 9.5g, of which saturates 1.9g; Cholesterol 127mg; Calcium 32mg; Fibre 1.2g; Sodium 56mg.

Flamenco eggs

This dish is a swirl of red, green, yellow and white – as colourful as the skirts of flamenco dancers. It uses whatever ingredients are available, for example, peas in spring or squash later in the year.

SERVES 4

30ml/2 tbsp olive oil
115g/4oz smoked bacon lardons
    or diced pancetta
2 frying chorizos, cubed
1 onion, chopped
2 garlic cloves, finely chopped
1 red and 1 green (bell) pepper,
    seeded and chopped
500g/1¼lb tomatoes, chopped
15–30ml/1–2 tbsp fino sherry
45ml/3 tbsp chopped fresh parsley
8 large (US extra large) eggs
salt, paprika and cayenne

FOR THE *MIGAS*
4 thick slices stale bread
oil, for frying
2 garlic cloves, bruised

1 Preheat the oven to 180°C/350°F/Gas 4. Warm four individual baking dishes.

2 Heat the oil in a frying pan and fry the bacon or pancetta and chorizos, to give off their fat. Add the onion and garlic and cook gently until softened, stirring. Add the peppers and tomatoes and cook until reduced, stirring occasionally. Add some paprika and sherry.

3 Divide the mixture evenly among the baking dishes. Sprinkle with parsley. Swirl the eggs together with a fork and season well with salt and cayenne. Pour over the mixture. Bake the eggs and vegetables for 8 minutes, or until the eggs are just set.

4 Meanwhile make the *migas*. Cut the crusts off the bread and reduce to crumbs in a food processor.

5 Heat plenty of oil in a frying pan over a high heat, add the garlic cloves for a few moments to flavour it, then discard them. Throw in the crumbs and brown quickly, scooping them out on to kitchen paper. Season with a little salt and paprika, then sprinkle around the edge of the eggs to serve.

Nutritional information per portion: Energy 592kcal/2464kJ; Protein 26.6g; Carbohydrate 30.4g, of which sugars 12g; Fat 41.1g, of which saturates 11.8g; Cholesterol 416mg; Calcium 155mg; Fibre 4.1g; Sodium 1150mg.

Scrambled eggs with prawns

The Spanish distinguish between a revuelto, *which uses softly-set scrambled eggs, and the more solid tortilla that is cooked until set. This* revuelto de gambas *is a good way of using shellfish.*

SERVES 4

1 bunch spring onions (scallions)
25g/1oz/2 tbsp butter
30ml/2 tbsp oil
150g/5oz shelled prawns (shrimp)
8 large (US extra large) eggs
30ml/2 tbsp milk
45ml/3 tbsp chopped fresh parsley
salt and ground black pepper
crusty bread, to serve

1 Chop the white of the spring onions and reserve, keeping it separate from 30ml/2 tbsp of the green tops.

2 Heat the butter and oil in a large frying pan. Add the spring onion white and cook briefly. Add the prawns and heat through. (If the prawns are raw, then cook them for 2 minutes.)

3 Beat the eggs with the milk and then season. Turn the heat to medium-high and pour the egg mixture over the prawns. Cook for about 2 minutes, stirring with a wooden spoon.

4 Sprinkle with parsley and spring onion greens. Divide among four plates and serve immediately with crusty bread.

Nutritional information per portion: Energy 285kcal/1182kJ; Protein 20.2g; Carbohydrate 1.5g, of which sugars 1.4g; Fat 22.4g, of which saturates 7.3g; Cholesterol 467mg; Calcium 129mg; Fibre 1g; Sodium 258mg.

Scrambled eggs with spring asparagus

Revuelto de espárragos is one of those delicious egg dishes that show off new green spring vegetables to perfection. Tender fresh asparagus and mangetouts are perfect partners to the eggs.

SERVES 4

1 bunch thin asparagus
30–45ml/2–3 tbsp mangetouts (snow peas)
8 large (US extra large) eggs
30ml/2 tbsp milk
50g/2oz/¼ cup butter
salt and ground black pepper
sweet paprika, for dusting

1 Prepare the asparagus. Using a sharp knife, cut off and discard any hard stems. Cut the stems, keeping the tips separate. Shell some of the fatter mangetout pods, to extract the peas, and cut the pods into strips, if you like.

2 Put the stems into a pan of boiling water and simmer for 4 minutes. Add the asparagus tips, and cook for another 6 minutes. If including some pea pod strips, cook them for 2 minutes. Break the eggs into a bowl and beat together with the milk, salt and black pepper.

3 Melt the butter in a frying pan and pour in the eggs, scrambling them by pulling the cooked outsides to the middle with a wooden spoon. When the eggs are almost cooked, drain the asparagus and pea pod strips, if using, and stir into the eggs. Sprinkle the peas over the top, dust with paprika and serve.

Nutritional information per portion: Energy 262kcal/1085kJ; Protein 14.9g; Carbohydrate 2.2g, of which sugars 1.4g; Fat 21.9g, of which saturates 9.7g; Cholesterol 407mg; Calcium 78mg; Fibre 1.4g; Sodium 217mg.

Pan-fried ham and vegetables with eggs

Little vegetable dishes, and ones that contain ham or eggs, or both, are the backbone of the Spanish supper scene. This delicious dish is easy to make and it is hearty enough to serve as a meal in itself with a simple salad.

SERVES 4

30ml/2 tbsp olive oil
1 onion, roughly chopped
2 garlic cloves, finely chopped
175g/6oz cooked ham
225g/8oz courgettes (zucchini)
1 red (bell) pepper, seeded and
    thinly sliced
1 yellow (bell) pepper, seeded and
    thinly sliced

10ml/2 tsp paprika
400g/14oz can chopped tomatoes
15ml/1 tbsp sun-dried tomato paste
4 large (US extra large) eggs
115g/4oz/1 cup coarsely grated
    Cheddar cheese
salt and ground black pepper
crusty bread, to serve

1 Heat the olive oil in a deep frying pan. Add the onion and garlic and cook for 4 minutes, stirring frequently.

2 Meanwhile, cut the cooked ham and courgettes into 5cm/2in batons.

3 Add the courgettes and peppers to the pan and cook over a medium heat for 3–4 minutes.

4 Stir in the paprika, tomatoes, tomato paste, ham and seasoning. Bring to a simmer and cook over a gentle heat for 15 minutes.

5 Reduce the heat to low. Make four wells in the tomato mixture, break an egg into each and season. Cook over a gentle heat until the white begins to set. Preheat the grill (broiler). Sprinkle the cheese over and grill (broil) for about 5 minutes until the eggs are set. Serve with crusty bread.

Nutritional information per portion: Energy 357kcal/1487kJ; Protein 24.8g; Carbohydrate 12.2g, of which sugars 10.7g; Fat 23.1g, of which saturates 9.4g; Cholesterol 244mg; Calcium 280mg; Fibre 3.1g; Sodium 817mg.

Vegetables

Salads start the meal in summer, and typify Spain's attitude to cooking, using fresh, local seasonal ingredients. Vegetable dishes are inventive too, eaten as tapas, a course on their own, or perhaps as a supper. Vegetables and salads are often embellished with chorizo, bacon lardons, tuna or hard-boiled eggs to add flavour and make a more substantial dish.

Ensaladilla

Known as Russian salad elsewhere, this "salad of little things" became extremely popular during the Spanish Civil War in the 1930s, when more expensive ingredients were scarce.

SERVES 4

8 new potatoes, scrubbed and quartered
1 large carrot, diced
115g/4oz fine green beans, cut into
    2cm/³⁄₄in lengths
75g/3oz/³⁄₄ cup peas
¹⁄₂ Spanish onion, chopped
4 cornichons or small gherkins, sliced
1 small red (bell) pepper, seeded and diced
50g/2oz/¹⁄₂ cup pitted black olives
15ml/1 tbsp drained pickled capers
15ml/1 tbsp freshly squeezed lemon juice
30ml/2 tbsp chopped fennel or parsley
salt and ground black pepper

FOR THE AIOLI
2 garlic cloves, finely chopped
2.5ml/¹⁄₂ tsp salt
150ml/¹⁄₄ pint/²⁄₃ cup mayonnaise

1 To make the aioli, crush the garlic with the salt in a mortar and whisk or stir into the mayonnaise.

2 Cook the potatoes and diced carrot in a pan of boiling lightly salted water for 5–8 minutes until almost tender. Add the beans and peas to the pan and cook for 2 minutes, or until all the vegetables are tender. Drain well.

3 Put the vegetables into a large bowl. Add the onion, cornichons or gherkins, red pepper, olives and capers. Stir in the aioli and season to taste with the black pepper and the lemon juice.

4 Toss the vegetables and aioli together until well combined, check the seasoning and chill well. Serve garnished with fennel or parsley.

Nutritional information per portion: Energy 494kcal/2045kJ; Protein 5.1g; Carbohydrate 25.6g, of which sugars 8.1g; Fat 42g, of which saturates 6.3g; Cholesterol 28mg; Calcium 60mg; Fibre 4.5g; Sodium 191mg.

Charred artichokes with lemon oil dip

Young artichokes, alcachofas, *are cooked over the first barbecues of the summer. However, they are also very good roasted in the oven.*

SERVES 2–4

15ml/1 tbsp lemon juice or white
  wine vinegar
2 globe artichokes
45ml/3 tbsp olive oil
sea salt
sprigs of fresh flat leaf parsley,
  to garnish

FOR THE LEMON OIL DIP
12 garlic cloves, unpeeled
1 lemon
45ml/3 tbsp extra virgin olive oil

1 Preheat the oven to 200°C/400°F/ Gas 6. Stir the lemon juice or the vinegar into a bowl of cold water.

2 Cut each artichoke lengthways into wedges. Pull the hairy choke out from the centre of each wedge and drop the wedges into the acidulated water.

3 Drain the artichokes and place in a roasting pan with the garlic cloves. Toss in the oil. Sprinkle with salt and roast for 40 minutes, stirring once or twice, until the artichokes are tender.

4 Meanwhile, make the dip. Pare away two strips of rind from the lemon and scrape away any pith. Place the rind in a pan with water to cover. Simmer for 5 minutes, then drain, refresh in cold water and chop roughly.

5 Arrange the artichokes on a plate and set aside to cool for 5 minutes. Flatten the garlic cloves so that the flesh pops out of the skins. Transfer the garlic flesh to a bowl, mash to a purée then add the lemon rind. Squeeze the juice from the lemon, then, using a fork, whisk in the olive oil and lemon juice.

6 Serve the artichokes warm, garnished with the parsley and accompanied with the dip.

Nutritional information per portion: Energy 166kcal/684kJ; Protein 1.4g; Carbohydrate 2.7g, of which sugars 0.9g; Fat 16.7g, of which saturates 2.4g; Cholesterol 0mg; Calcium 33mg; Fibre 1.3g; Sodium 46mg.

Mushroom, bean and chorizo salad

This really simple salad can be served as an accompaniment to plain fish or chicken dishes, or with crusty bread as a hearty lunch or supper dish. The combination of spicy sausage, beans and mushrooms is delicious.

SERVES 4

225g/8oz shelled broad (fava) beans
175g/6oz frying chorizo
60ml/4 tbsp extra virgin olive oil
225g/8oz/3 cups brown cap (cremini) mushrooms, sliced
60ml/4 tbsp chopped fresh chives
salt and ground black pepper

1 Cook the broad beans in a pan of salted boiling water for 7–8 minutes. Drain and refresh under cold water.

2 Remove the skin from the sausage. If it doesn't peel off easily, score along the length of the sausage with a sharp knife first. Cut the chorizo into small chunks. Heat the oil in a small pan, add the chorizo and cook for 2–3 minutes.

3 Put the sliced mushrooms in a bowl and add the chorizo and oil. Toss to combine then leave to cool.

4 If the beans are large, peel away the tough outer skins. Stir the beans and half the chives into the mushroom mixture, and season to taste. Serve at room temperature, garnished with the remaining chives.

Nutritional information per portion: Energy 166kcal/684kJ; Protein 1.4g; Carbohydrate 2.7g, of which sugars 0.9g; Fat 16.7g, of which saturates 2.4g; Cholesterol 0mg; Calcium 33mg; Fibre 1.3g; Sodium 46mg.

Avocado, orange and almond salad

In Andalusia, avocados have become one of the big cash crops, replacing many orange orchards. In this salad, ensalada de aguacates, the smooth, creamy avocados combine perfectly with local oranges and almonds.

SERVES 4

2–3 oranges
2 ripe tomatoes
2 small avocados
60ml/4 tbsp extra virgin olive oil
30ml/2 tbsp lemon juice
15ml/1 tbsp chopped fresh parsley
1 small onion, cut into rings
25g/1oz/1/4 cup split, toasted almonds
10–12 black olives
salt and ground black pepper

1 Peel the oranges and slice them into thick rounds. Plunge the tomatoes into boiling water for 30 seconds, then refresh in cold water. Peel away the skins, cut the tomatoes into quarters, remove the seeds and chop them roughly. Cut the avocados in half, remove the stones (pits) and carefully peel away the skin. Cut into chunks.

2 Mix together the olive oil, lemon juice and parsley. Season with salt and pepper, then toss the avocados and tomatoes in half of the dressing.

3 Arrange the oranges on a plate and add the onion rings. Drizzle with the remaining dressing. Spoon over avocados, tomatoes, almonds and olives and serve. .

Nutritional information per portion: Energy 295kcal/1224kJ; Protein 4g; Carbohydrate 12.5g, of which sugars 11.6g; Fat 25.8g, of which saturates 4.2g; Cholesterol 0mg; Calcium 85mg; Fibre 5g; Sodium 295mg.

La calçotada

Spring onions – calçot in Spanish – have their own festival in the province of Tarragona. It is a day to mark the return of better weather, and in the past, the onions were barbecued in the fields.

SERVES 6

3 bunches of plump spring onions
(scallions), or Chinese green onions,
which are about 2.5cm/1in across
the bulb
olive oil, for brushing

FOR THE ROMESCO SAUCE

2–3 *ñoras* or other mild dried red chillies,
such as Mexican *anchos* or *guajillos*
1 large red (bell) pepper, halved
and seeded
2 large tomatoes, halved and seeded
4–6 large garlic cloves, unpeeled
75–90ml/5–6 tbsp olive oil
25g/1oz/¼ cup hazelnuts, blanched
4 slices French bread, each about
2cm/¾in thick
15ml/1 tbsp sherry vinegar
squeeze of lemon juice (optional)

1 Soak the dried chillies in hot water for about 30 minutes. Preheat the oven to 220°C/425°F/Gas 7. Place the pepper, tomatoes and garlic on a baking sheet and drizzle with 15ml/1 tbsp olive oil. Roast, uncovered, for 30–40 minutes, until the pepper is blistered and blackened and the garlic is soft. Cool slightly, then peel the pepper, tomatoes and garlic.

2 Heat the remaining oil in a small frying pan and fry the hazelnuts until lightly browned, then transfer them to a plate. Fry the bread in the same oil until light brown on both sides, then transfer to the plate with the nuts and leave to cool. Reserve the oil from cooking.

3 Drain the chillies, discard as many of their seeds as you can, then place the chillies in a food processor. Add the red pepper halves, tomatoes, garlic, hazelnuts and bread chunks together with the reserved olive oil. Add the vinegar and process to a paste. Check the seasoning and thin the sauce with a little more oil or lemon juice, if necessary. Set aside.

4 Trim the roots from the spring onions or trim the Chinese onion leaves so that they are about 15–18cm/6–7in long. Brush with oil. Heat an oiled ridged griddle and cook the onions for about 2 minutes on each side, turning once and brushing with oil. Serve at once with the sauce.

Nutritional information per portion: Energy 214kcal/896kJ; Protein 5.2g; Carbohydrate 21g, of which sugars 5.3g; Fat 12.8g, of which saturates 1.7g; Cholesterol 0mg; Calcium 64mg; Fibre 2.8g; Sodium 173mg.

Stewed aubergine

The Arabs introduced this vegetable-fruit to Andalusia, where it was cooked with the Arab flavourings of cumin and garlic. This is a modern version of **berenjena guisada,** *with red wine.*

SERVES 4

1 large aubergine (eggplant)
60–90ml/4–6 tbsp olive oil
2 shallots, thinly sliced
4 tomatoes, quartered
2 garlic cloves, thinly sliced
60ml/4 tbsp red wine
30ml/2 tbsp chopped fresh parsley,
    plus extra to garnish
30–45ml/2–3 tbsp extra virgin olive oil
    (if serving cold)
salt and ground black pepper

1 Slice the aubergine into 1cm/1/2in rounds. Place them in a large colander and sprinkle with 5–10ml/1–2 tsp salt. Leave to drain for 30 minutes.

2 Rinse the aubergine slices well, then press between several layers of kitchen paper to remove any excess liquid.

3 Heat 30ml/2 tbsp of the oil in a large frying pan until smoking. Add a single layer of aubergine slices and fry, turning once, until golden brown. Remove to a plate covered with kitchen paper to drain. Heat more oil and fry the second batch in the same way.

4 Heat 15ml/1 tbsp of oil in a pan and cook the shallots for 5 minutes until golden. Cut the aubergine into strips. Add, with the tomatoes, garlic and wine. Cover and simmer for 30 minutes.

5 Stir in the parsley, and check the seasonings. Sprinkle with a little more parsley and serve hot. To serve cold, dribble a little extra virgin olive oil over the dish before it goes on the table.

Nutritional information per portion: Energy 197kcal/816kJ; Protein 2g; Carbohydrate 7.3g, of which sugars 6.7g; Fat 17.3g, of which saturates 2.6g; Cholesterol 0mg; Calcium 23mg; Fibre 3.5g; Sodium 15mg.

Braised cabbage with chorizo

Cabbages – berzas – mark the landscape in Galicia, where the huge vegetables grow more than hip high. They are popularly cooked in stews in the many mountain regions of the south, and are frequently served with chickpeas or sausages, as in this recipe.

SERVES 4

50g/2oz/¼ cup butter
5ml/1 tsp coriander seeds
225g/8oz green cabbage, shredded
2 garlic cloves, finely chopped
**50g/2oz cured chorizo sausage,
    roughly chopped**
60ml/4 tbsp dry sherry or white wine
salt and ground black pepper

1 Melt the butter in a large frying pan, add the coriander seeds and cook for 1 minute. Add the shredded cabbage to the pan with the chopped garlic and chorizo. Stir-fry gently for 5 minutes.

2 Add the sherry or wine and plenty of salt and pepper to the pan. Cover and cook for 15–20 minutes until the cabbage is tender. Check the seasoning, adding more if necessary, and then serve.

Nutritional information per portion: Energy 163kcal/673kJ; Protein 2.1g; Carbohydrate 4.6g, of which sugars 3.3g; Fat 13.4g, of which saturates 7.8g; Cholesterol 32mg; Calcium 37mg; Fibre 1.3g; Sodium 183mg.

Broad beans with bacon

This dish is associated with Ronda, in southern Spain, the home of bull fighting, where broad beans are fed to the bulls to build them up. It is also found elsewhere in Spain where it is known as habas españolas. *If you have time, remove the outer dull skins from the broad beans.*

SERVES 4

30ml/2 tbsp olive oil
1 small onion, finely chopped
1 garlic clove, finely chopped
50g/2oz rindless smoked streaky (fatty)
    bacon, roughly chopped
225g/8oz broad (fava) beans, thawed
    if frozen
5ml/1 tsp paprika
15ml/1 tbsp sweet sherry
salt and ground black pepper

1 Heat the olive oil in a large frying pan or sauté pan. Add the chopped onion, garlic and bacon and fry over a high heat for about 5 minutes, stirring frequently, until the onion is softened and the bacon browned.

2 Add the beans and paprika to the pan and stir-fry for 1 minute. Add the sherry, lower the heat, cover and cook for 5–10 minutes until the beans are tender. Season with salt and pepper and serve hot or warm.

Nutritional information per portion: Energy 139kcal/577kJ; Protein 6.8g; Carbohydrate 8.2g, of which sugars 1.6g; Fat 9g, of which saturates 1.9g; Cholesterol 8mg; Calcium 38mg; Fibre 3.9g; Sodium 163mg.

Amanida

The word amanida *is Catalan for an arranged salad that includes fish, meat and vegetables in equal proportions. These salads can be a wonder to behold, but are also simple to make.*

SERVES 6

1 lolla green lettuce
50g/2oz cured, sliced chorizo or in a piece
 skinned and diced
4 thin slices Serrano ham
130g/4½oz can sardines in oil, drained
130g/4½oz can tuna steak in oil, drained
8 canned white asparagus spears, drained
2–3 canned palm hearts, drained
115g/4oz/²/₃ cup tiny arbequina olives
115g/4oz/²/₃ cup big gordas or queen
 olives, preferably purplish ones

10 medium tomatoes
15ml/1 tbsp chopped fresh parsley,
 to garnish

FOR THE VINAIGRETTE
1 garlic clove, split lengthways
30ml/2 tbsp sherry vinegar
30ml/2 tbsp red wine vinegar
60ml/4 tbsp olive oil
60ml/4 tbsp extra virgin olive oil
salt and ground black pepper

1 Make the vinaigrette. Wipe the cut side of the garlic round a large bowl, then discard. Whisk the other ingredients together in the bowl.

2 Break the stem ends off eight lettuce leaves, dip the leaves into the vinaigrette and arrange them around a large serving plate.

3 Position the chorizo slices or dice on one side of the plate. Roll the ham and arrange opposite. Drain and blot the fish, then arrange across the plate in a cross. Put the asparagus, spears outwards, and the palm hearts (split lengthways), on opposite sides of the plate. Pile the olives in the spaces.

4 Put the tomatoes in a bowl and pour over boiling water. Leave to stand for 10 minutes, then drain. Peel and quarter six of the tomatoes and cut out the centres. Arrange the tomatoes, round side up, in the centre of the plate to make a flower shape. Brush vinaigrette dressing over the tomatoes, palm hearts and asparagus and season lightly. Sprinkle the parsley on the tomatoes and white vegetables. Serve at room temperature.

Nutritional information per portion: Energy 638kcal/2671kJ; Protein 74.6g; Carbohydrate 9.8g, of which sugars 9.8g; Fat 33.7g, of which saturates 7.3g; Cholesterol 218mg; Calcium 183mg; Fibre 3.1g; Sodium 4618mg.

Patatas bravas

There are several variations on this chilli and potato dish, but the most important thing is the spicing, which is made hotter still by adding vinegar. The name bravas *implies that the potatoes are so hot that it is manly to eat them.*

SERVES 4

675g/1¹/₂lb small new potatoes
75ml/5 tbsp olive oil
2 garlic cloves, sliced
3 dried chillies, seeded and chopped
2.5ml/¹/₂ tsp ground cumin
10ml/2 tsp paprika
30ml/2 tbsp red or white wine vinegar
1 red or green (bell) pepper, seeded
   and sliced
coarse sea salt, for sprinkling (optional)

1 Scrub the potatoes and put them into a pan of salted water. Bring to the boil and cook for 10 minutes, or until almost tender. Drain and leave to cool slightly. Peel, if you like, then cut into chunks.

2 Heat the oil in a frying or sauté pan and fry the potatoes, turning them frequently, until golden.

3 Meanwhile, crush together the garlic cloves, the chillies and cumin using a mortar and pestle. Mix the paste with the paprika and wine vinegar, then add to the potatoes with the pepper and cook, stirring, for 2 minutes. Sprinkle with salt, if using, and serve hot as a tapas dish or cold as a side dish.

Nutritional information per portion: Energy 256kcal/1070kJ; Protein 3.3g; Carbohydrate 30g, of which sugars 4.9g; Fat 14.4g, of which saturates 2.2g; Cholesterol 0mg; Calcium 14mg; Fibre 2.4g; Sodium 20mg.

Escalivada

The Catalan name of this celebrated dish means "baked over embers" and, like many other barbecue dishes, it transfers very successfully to the oven. Cooking the vegetables in this way brings out their flavour magnificently.

SERVES 4

2–3 courgettes (zucchini)
1 large fennel bulb
1 Spanish onion
2 large red (bell) peppers
450g/1lb butternut squash
6 whole garlic cloves, unpeeled
75ml/5 tbsp olive oil
juice of 1/2 lemon
pinch of cumin seeds, crushed
4 sprigs fresh thyme
4 medium tomatoes, halved
salt and ground black pepper

1 Preheat the oven to 220°C/425°F/Gas 7. Cut the courgettes lengthways into four pieces. Cut the fennel into similar-sized wedges. Slice the onion lengthways into chunks. Halve and seed the peppers, and slice thickly lengthways. Cut the squash into thick chunks. Smash the garlic cloves with the flat of a knife, but leave the skins on.

2 Choose a roasting pan into which all the vegetables will fit in one layer. Put in all the vegetables except the tomatoes. Mix together the olive oil and lemon juice. Pour over the vegetables and toss them. Sprinkle with the cumin seeds, salt and pepper and tuck in the thyme sprigs. Roast for 20 minutes.

3 Gently stir the vegetables in the oil and add the tomatoes. Cook for a further 15 minutes, or until the vegetables are tender and slightly charred around the edges.

Nutritional information per portion: Energy 209kcal/864kJ; Protein 4.6g; Carbohydrate 14.3g, of which sugars 13g; Fat 15.1g, of which saturates 2.4g; Cholesterol 0mg; Calcium 86mg; Fibre 5.6g; Sodium 17mg.

Stuffed tomatoes and peppers

Colourful peppers and tomatoes make perfect containers for a simple rice, nut and herb stuffing. The vegetables become deliciously sweet and juicy when baked. Serve **tomates y pimientas rellenos** *as a substantial appetizer or a supper dish.*

SERVES 4

2 large tomatoes
1 green (bell) pepper
1 yellow or orange (bell) pepper
75ml/5 tbsp olive oil
2 onions, finely chopped
2 garlic cloves, finely chopped
75g/3oz/¾ cup almonds, chopped
175g/6oz/1½ cups cooked rice, or
   75g/3oz/scant ½ cup long grain rice,
   cooked and drained
30ml/2 tbsp Malaga raisins or muscatels,
   soaked in hot water
30ml/2 tbsp chopped fresh mint
45ml/3 tbsp chopped fresh flat leaf
   parsley, plus extra to garnish
salt and ground black pepper

1 Preheat the oven to 190°C/375°F/Gas 5. Cut the tomatoes in half and scoop out the pulp and seeds.

2 Put the tomato halves on kitchen paper with the cut sides down and leave to drain. Roughly chop the centres and seeds and place in a bowl.

3 Halve the peppers, leaving the cores intact. Scoop out the seeds. Brush the peppers with 15ml/1 tbsp of the oil.

4 Fry the onions and garlic in 30ml/2 tbsp oil. Stir in most of the almonds. Add the rice, tomato pulp, drained raisins, mint and 30ml/2 tbsp parsley. Season well, then spoon the mixture into the vegetable cases.

5 Bake uncovered for 20 minutes. Finely chop the remaining almonds and parsley in a food processor and sprinkle over the top. Drizzle with 15–30ml/1–2 tbsp olive oil. Return to the oven and bake for a further 20 minutes, or until turning golden. Serve, garnished with more chopped parsley.

Nutritional information per portion: Energy 365kcal/1522kJ; Protein 7.1g; Carbohydrate 28.6g, of which sugars 13.7g; Fat 25.5g, of which saturates 3.1g; Cholesterol 0mg; Calcium 95mg; Fibre 3.7g; Sodium 20mg.

Mojete

The Spanish love to scoop up cooked vegetables with bread, and the name of this dish, which is derived from the word meaning to dip, reflects that. Peppers, tomatoes and onions are baked together to make a colourful, soft vegetable dish that is studded with olives.

SERVES 8

2 red (bell) peppers
2 yellow (bell) peppers
1 red onion, sliced
2 garlic cloves, halved
50g/2oz/¼ cup black olives
6 large ripe tomatoes, quartered
5ml/1 tsp soft light brown sugar
45ml/3 tbsp amontillado sherry
3–4 fresh rosemary sprigs
30ml/2 tbsp olive oil
salt and ground black pepper
fresh bread, to serve

1 Halve the peppers and remove the seeds. Cut each pepper lengthways into 12 strips. Preheat the oven to 200°C/400°F/Gas 6.

2 Place the peppers, onion, garlic, olives and tomatoes in a large roasting pan.

3 Sprinkle the vegetables with the sugar, then pour in the sherry. Season well with salt and pepper, cover with foil and bake for 45 minutes.

4 Remove the foil from the pan and stir the mixture well. Add the rosemary sprigs and drizzle with the olive oil. Return the pan to the oven and cook for a further 30 minutes, uncovered, until the vegetables are very tender. Serve hot or cold with chunks of fresh crusty bread.

Nutritional information per portion: Energy 75kcal/313kJ; Protein 1.3g; Carbohydrate 7.5g, of which sugars 7.2g; Fat 3.9g, of which saturates 0.6g; Cholesterol 0mg; Calcium 17mg; Fibre 2g; Sodium 151mg.

Marinated mushrooms

Champiñones en escabeche *is a good way to serve mushrooms in summer, and makes a refreshing alternative to the ever-popular mushrooms fried in garlic. Serve with plenty of crusty bread to mop up the delicious juices.*

SERVES 4

30ml/2 tbsp olive oil
1 small onion, very finely chopped
1 garlic clove, finely chopped
15ml/1 tbsp tomato purée (paste)
50ml/2fl oz/¼ cup amontillado sherry
50ml/2fl oz/¼ cup water
2 cloves
225g/8oz/3 cups button (white) mushrooms, trimmed
salt and ground black pepper
chopped fresh parsley, to garnish

1 Heat the oil in a pan. Add the onion and garlic and cook until soft. Stir in the tomato purée, sherry, water and cloves, and season to taste. Bring to the boil, cover and simmer gently for 45 minutes. Add more water if it becomes too dry.

2 Add the mushrooms to the pan, then cover and simmer for about 5 minutes. Remove from the heat and allow to cool, still covered. Chill in the refrigerator overnight. Serve the mushrooms cold, sprinkled with the chopped fresh parsley.

Nutritional information per portion: Energy 80kcal/329kJ; Protein 1.4g; Carbohydrate 2.1g, of which sugars 1.7g; Fat 5.8g, of which saturates 0.9g; Cholesterol 0mg; Calcium 9mg; Fibre 0.9g; Sodium 14mg.

Spinach with raisins and pine nuts

Raisins and pine nuts are frequent partners in Spanish recipes, a combination that was first introduced by the Moors. Here, tossed with wilted spinach and croûtons, they make a delicious snack or main course accompaniment.

SERVES 4

50g/2oz/¹/₃ cup raisins, preferably
   Malaga raisins
1 thick slice white bread
45ml/3 tbsp olive oil
25g/1oz/¹/₄ cup pine nuts
500g/1¹/₄lb young spinach,
   stalks removed
2 garlic cloves, finely chopped
salt and ground black pepper

1 Put the raisins in a small bowl and pour over enough boiling water to cover. Leave the raisins to soak for about 10 minutes, then drain well.

2 Cut off the crusts from the white bread and cut into cubes. Heat 30ml/2 tbsp of the oil in a frying pan and fry the cubes of bread until golden. Drain.

3 Heat the remaining oil in the pan. Gently fry the pine nuts until just colouring. Add the spinach and garlic and cook quickly, turning the spinach until it has just wilted.

4 Add the raisins and season lightly with salt and pepper. Transfer to a warmed dish. Sprinkle with the croûtons and serve immediately.

Nutritional information per portion: Energy 206kcal/855kJ; Protein 5.8g; Carbohydrate 15.5g, of which sugars 11.1g; Fat 13.8g, of which saturates 1.6g; Cholesterol 0mg; Calcium 228mg; Fibre 3.4g; Sodium 218mg.

Menestra

This vegetable dish, which contains an assortment of young, new vegetables, is generally eaten to celebrate the arrival of spring.

SERVES 6

15ml/1 tbsp olive oil

115g/4oz streaky (fatty) bacon
   lardons or diced pancetta

1 onion, chopped

3 garlic cloves, finely chopped

90ml/6 tbsp chopped fresh parsley

175ml/6fl oz/³⁄₄ cup dry white wine

150g/5oz green beans

200g/7oz bunched young carrots

6 small new potatoes, scrubbed

300ml/10fl oz/1¼ cups chicken stock

1 corn cob, kernels removed (optional)

200g/7oz/2 cups peas

50g/2oz mangetouts (snow peas)

salt and ground black pepper

2 hard-boiled eggs, chopped, to garnish

1 Heat the oil in a large, heavy pan and fry the bacon or pancetta over a gentle heat for about 5 minutes, or until it crisps. Remove with a slotted spoon and reserve. Add the onion to the pan and cook in the bacon fat until softened, adding the garlic towards the end.

2 Remove the cooked onion to a food processor, add 30ml/2 tbsp of the chopped parsley and purée with a little of the white wine.

3 Prepare the vegetables. Cut the beans into short lengths, and the carrots to the same size. Bring a pan of salted water to the boil and add the potatoes. Cook for about 10 minutes. Add the carrots to the pan of potatoes, and cook for a further 5 minutes.

4 Meanwhile, return the bacon to the other pan and add the stock. Put in the beans, corn kernels and peas and lay the mangetouts over the top. Half cover the pan and leave to simmer for 5–10 minutes, until the vegetables are just cooked. Drain the potatoes and carrots and add them to the pan.

5 Add the rest of the wine and the onion purée to the pan, warming the liquid and turning the vegetables gently with a wooden spoon. Check the seasoning, adding more if necessary, and serve with the juices. Garnish with chopped egg and the remaining parsley.

Nutritional information per portion: Energy 207kcal/865kJ; Protein 8.1g; Carbohydrate 23.4g, of which sugars 9.6g; Fat 7.6g, of which saturates 2.1g; Cholesterol 12mg; Calcium 68mg; Fibre 5.5g; Sodium 274mg.

Pisto manchego

A rich-flavoured and simple summer vegetable dish, from the poorest and hottest part of Spain, La Mancha. It may be eaten hot or as a substantial salad, with canned tuna, or hard-boiled eggs.

SERVES 4

45ml/3 tbsp olive oil

2 Spanish onions, thinly sliced

3 garlic cloves, finely chopped

3 large green (bell) peppers, seeded and chopped

3 large courgettes (zucchini), thinly sliced

5 large ripe tomatoes or 800g/1¾lb can tomatoes, with juice

60ml/4 tbsp chopped fresh parsley

2 hard-boiled eggs, chopped (optional)

30ml/2 tbsp extra virgin olive oil (if serving cold)

salt and ground black pepper

1 Heat the oil in a large, heavy pan and cook the sliced onions and garlic gently, until they are soft.

2 Add the peppers, courgettes and tomatoes. Season and cook gently over a low heat for 20 minutes to blend the flavours.

3 Stir in 30ml/2 tbsp parsley and serve hot, if wished, topped with chopped hard-boiled egg, if using, and more parsley. To serve cold, check the seasoning, adding more if needed, and sprinkle with a little extra virgin olive oil before adding the parsley garnish.

Nutritional information per portion: Energy 196kcal/812kJ; Protein 6.2g; Carbohydrate 21.3g, of which sugars 18.5g; Fat 10g, of which saturates 1.6g; Cholesterol 0mg; Calcium 109mg; Fibre 6.4g; Sodium 25mg.

Lentils with mushrooms and anis

The plains of Castile produce lentils for the whole of Europe. Locally they are weekly fare. In this recipe, lentejas con champiñones, *they are flavoured with another regional product, anis spirit.*

SERVES 4

30ml/2 tbsp olive oil

1 large onion, sliced

2 garlic cloves, finely chopped

250g/9oz/3 cups brown cap (cremini) mushrooms, sliced

150g/5oz/generous 1/2 cup brown or green lentils

4 tomatoes, cut in eighths

1 bay leaf

25g/1oz/1/2 cup chopped fresh parsley

30ml/2 tbsp anis spirit or anisette

salt, paprika and black pepper

1 Heat the oil in a large, heavy pan. Add the sliced onion and fry gently over a low heat, with the garlic, until softened but not browned.

2 Add the sliced mushrooms and stir to combine with the onion and garlic. Continue cooking, stirring gently, for a couple of minutes.

3 Add the lentils, tomato wedges and bay leaf with 175ml/6fl oz/ 3/4 cup water. Simmer gently, covered, for 30–40 minutes until the lentils are soft, and the liquid has almost disappeared.

4 Stir in the chopped parsley and anis. Season with salt, paprika and black pepper.

Nutritional information per portion: Energy 242kcal/1018kJ; Protein 12.5g; Carbohydrate 29.8g, of which sugars 9.5g; Fat 7.2g, of which saturates 1g; Cholesterol 0mg; Calcium 83mg; Fibre 6.9g; Sodium 23mg.

Rice and pasta

Paella – that glorious combination of saffron rice, with shellfish, chicken or rabbit – is probably the dish most commonly associated with Spain. But there are many more festival and family dishes that combine rice with vegetables. Pasta is a 500-year-old tradition, and comes in the same versatile combinations as the rice.

Artichoke rice cakes with Manchego

These unusual little croquetas contain artichoke in the rice mixture, and they break open to reveal a melting cheese centre. Manchego is made from sheep's milk and has a tart flavour that goes wonderfully with the delicate taste of the rice cakes.

SERVES 6

1 large globe artichoke
50g/2oz/¼ cup butter
1 small onion, finely chopped
1 garlic clove, finely chopped
115g/4oz/²/₃ cup paella rice
450ml/¾ pint/scant 2 cups hot
   chicken stock
50g/2oz/²/₃ cup freshly grated
   Parmesan cheese
150g/5oz Manchego cheese, very
   finely diced
45–60ml/3–4 tbsp fine corn meal
olive oil, for frying
salt and ground black pepper
fresh flat leaf parsley, to garnish

1 Remove the heart of the artichoke and chop finely.

2 Melt the butter in a pan and fry the artichoke heart, onion and garlic for 5 minutes. Add the rice and cook for 1 minute.

3 Keeping the heat fairly high, gradually add the stock, stirring until the liquid has been absorbed and the rice is cooked – this should take about 20 minutes. Season well, then stir in the Parmesan cheese. Transfer the mixture to a bowl. Cool, cover and chill for 2 hours.

4 Spoon about 15ml/1 tbsp of the mixture into the palm of one hand, flatten slightly, and place a few pieces of diced cheese in the centre. Shape the rice around the cheese to make a small ball. Flatten slightly, then roll in the corn meal, shaking off any excess. Repeat with the remaining mixture to make 12 rice cakes.

5 Shallow fry the rice cakes in hot olive oil for 4–5 minutes until they are crisp and golden brown. Drain the rice cakes on kitchen paper and serve hot, garnished with flat leaf parsley.

Nutritional information per portion: Energy 354kcal/1469kJ; Protein 12g; Carbohydrate 21.8g, of which sugars 0.8g; Fat 23.6g, of which saturates 12.3g; Cholesterol 50mg; Calcium 299mg; Fibre 0.5g; Sodium 331mg.

Rice tortitas

Like miniature tortillas, these little rice pancakes are good served hot, either plain or with tomato sauce for dipping. They make an excellent scoop for any soft vegetable mixture or dip – a very Spanish way of eating.

SERVES 4

30ml/2 tbsp olive oil

115g/4oz/1 cup cooked long grain white rice

1 potato, grated

4 spring onions (scallions), thinly sliced

1 garlic clove, finely chopped

15ml/1 tbsp chopped fresh parsley

3 large (US extra large) eggs, beaten

2.5ml/¹/₂ tsp paprika

salt and ground black pepper

1 Heat half the olive oil in a large frying pan and stir-fry the rice, together with the potato, spring onions and garlic, over a high heat for 3 minutes until golden.

2 Put the rice and vegetable mixture into a bowl and stir in the parsley and eggs, with the paprika and plenty of salt and pepper. Mix well.

3 Heat the remaining oil in the frying pan and drop in large spoonfuls of the rice mixture, leaving space for spreading. Cook the *tortitas* for 1–2 minutes on each side until golden.

4 Drain the *tortitas* on kitchen paper and keep hot while cooking the remaining mixture. Serve hot.

Nutritional information per portion: Energy 185kcal/776kJ; Protein 6.8g; Carbohydrate 17.6g, of which sugars 1.2g; Fat 10.4g, of which saturates 2.1g; Cholesterol 143mg; Calcium 56mg; Fibre 1.3g; Sodium 63mg.

Moors and Christians

Moros y Cristianos is made in Valencia at the annual festival celebrating an ancient victory of the Christians over the Moors. The black beans represent the latter, and the white rice the former.

SERVES 6

400g/14oz/2 cups black beans, soaked
   overnight
1 onion
1 carrot
1 celery stick
1 garlic clove, finely chopped
1 bay leaf
1.75l/3 pints/2 cups water
5ml/1 tsp paprika
45ml/3 tbsp olive oil
juice of 1 orange
300g/11oz/1¹/₂ cups long grain rice
salt and cayenne pepper

FOR THE GARNISH

chopped fresh parsley
thin wedges of orange
sliced red onion

1 Put the beans in a pan with the onion, carrot, celery, garlic, bay leaf and water. Bring to the boil and cook rapidly for 10 minutes, then reduce the heat and simmer for 1 hour. Top up the water, if necessary. When the beans are almost tender, drain, discarding the vegetables and bay leaf. Return the beans to a clean pan.

2 Blend the paprika and oil with cayenne pepper to taste and stir into the beans with the orange juice. Top up with water, if necessary. Heat until barely simmering, then cover and cook for 15 minutes until the beans are tender. Remove from the heat and allow to stand for 15 minutes. Season with salt.

3 Cook the rice until tender. Drain, then pack into moulds and leave for 10 minutes. Transfer the rice to serving plates and arrange the beans around the edges. Garnish with the parsley, orange and red onion.

Nutritional information per portion: Energy 445kcal/1875kJ; Protein 19.7g; Carbohydrate 77.8g, of which sugars 3.2g; Fat 7g, of which saturates 1.1g; Cholesterol 0mg; Calcium 68mg; Fibre 5.6g; Sodium 12mg.

Simple rice salad

In this quick and easy side dish, rice and a selection of freshly chopped salad vegetables are served in a well-flavoured dressing to make a pretty, colourful salad.

SERVES 6

275g/10oz/1¹/₂ cups long grain rice

1 bunch spring onions (scallions), finely sliced

1 green (bell) pepper, seeded and finely diced

1 yellow (bell) pepper, seeded and finely diced

225g/8oz tomatoes, peeled, seeded and chopped

30ml/2 tbsp chopped fresh flat leaf parsley or coriander (cilantro)

FOR THE DRESSING

75ml/5 tbsp extra virgin olive oil

15ml/1 tbsp sherry vinegar

5ml/1 tsp strong Dijon mustard

salt and ground black pepper

1 Cook the rice in a large pan of lightly salted boiling water for 10–12 minutes, until tender but still *al dente*. Be careful not to overcook it.

2 Drain the rice well in a sieve (strainer), rinse thoroughly under cold running water and drain again. Leave the rice to cool completely.

3 Place the rice in a large serving bowl. Add the spring onions, peppers, tomatoes and parsley or coriander.

4 Make the dressing. Place all the ingredients in a screw-top jar, put the lid on and shake vigorously until well mixed. Stir the dressing into the rice and check the seasoning.

Nutritional information per portion: Energy 280kcal/1166kJ; Protein 4.9g; Carbohydrate 42.3g, of which sugars 5.5g; Fat 10g, of which saturates 1.4g; Cholesterol 0mg; Calcium 40mg; Fibre 2g; Sodium 34mg.

Paella Valenciana

A world-famous mixture of the finest Spanish ingredients, Valencia's paella contains chicken, shellfish and vegetables mixed in with succulent saffron rice.

SERVES 6–8

90ml/6 tbsp white wine

450g/1lb fresh mussels, scrubbed

115g/4oz/scant 1 cup small shelled broad (fava) beans

150g/5oz green beans, cut into short lengths

90ml/6 tbsp olive oil

6 small skinless, boneless chicken breast portions, cut into large pieces

150g/5oz pork fillet, cubed

6–8 large raw prawn (shrimp) tails, deveined, or 12 smaller raw prawns

2 onions, chopped

2–3 garlic cloves, finely chopped

1 red (bell) pepper, seeded and sliced

2 ripe tomatoes, peeled, seeded and chopped

60ml/4 tbsp chopped fresh parsley

900ml/1½ pints/3¾ cups chicken stock

pinch of saffron threads (0.25g), soaked in 30ml/2 tbsp hot water

350g/12oz/1¾ cups paella rice, washed and drained

225g/8oz frying chorizo, sliced

115g/4oz/1 cup peas

6–8 stuffed green olives, sliced

salt, paprika and black pepper

1 Heat the wine and add the mussels, discarding any that do not close when tapped. Cover and steam until opened. Reserve the liquid and mussels separately, discarding any that do not open.

2 Briefly cook the broad beans and green beans in boiling water, then drain. Pop the broad beans out of their skins.

3 Heat 45ml/3 tbsp oil in a large paella pan or wide flameproof casserole. Season the chicken with salt and paprika and fry, turning until browned on all sides. Reserve on a plate. Season the pork with salt and paprika. Add 15ml/1 tbsp oil and fry the seasoned pork until evenly browned. Reserve with the chicken. Fry the prawns briefly in the same pan, but reserve them separately.

4 Add the remaining oil to the pan and heat. Fry the onions and garlic for 3–4 minutes until golden brown. Add the red pepper, cook for 2–3 minutes, then stir in the chopped tomatoes and parsley and cook until thickened. If cooking in the oven, preheat to 190°C/375°F/Gas 5.

5 Stir the chicken stock, the reserved mussel liquid and the saffron liquid into the vegetables. Season well with salt and pepper and bring the mixture to the boil. When the liquid is bubbling, throw in all the rice. Stir once, then add the chicken pieces, pork, prawns, beans, chorizo and peas.

6 Transfer the pan to the oven and cook for 15–18 minutes until the rice is done. Alternatively, cook over medium-high heat for about 10 minutes. Then lower the heat and start to move the pan. A big pan needs to shift every 2–3 minutes, moving the edge of the pan round over the heat, then back to the centre. Cook until the rice is done – another 10–12 minutes.

7 Arrange the mussels and olives on top. Cover with a lid (or damp dishtowel) and leave to stand for 10 minutes, until all the liquid is absorbed. Serve straight from the pan.

COOK'S TIP
Traditionally, paella is cooked outdoors on a wide bed of hot charcoal. Indoors a big heat source such as a large hotplate or an oven is needed. Without this steady heat, the pan needs to be moved to cook the rice evenly.

Nutritional information per portion: Energy 712kcal/2978kJ; Protein 69.9g; Carbohydrate 48g, of which sugars 5.8g; Fat 26.1g, of which saturates 6.4g; Cholesterol 208mg; Calcium 98mg; Fibre 3.6g; Sodium 468mg.

Seafood paella

This is a great dish to serve on a special occasion as it looks spectacular.
A bed of scented rice is the perfect way to display a selection of seafood.

SERVES 4

45ml/3 tbsp olive oil
1 Spanish onion, chopped
2 large garlic cloves, chopped
150g/5oz frying chorizo, sliced
300g/11oz small squid, cleaned
1 red (bell) pepper, cut into strips
4 tomatoes, peeled, seeded and diced,
    or 200g/7oz can tomatoes
500ml/17fl oz/2¼ cups chicken stock,
    plus a little extra
105ml/7 tbsp dry white wine
200g/7oz/1 cup paella rice

pinch of saffron threads (0.2g), crumbled
150g/5oz/generous 1 cup peas
12 large cooked prawns (shrimp), in the
    shell ,or 8 peeled scampi (extra large
    shrimp)
450g/1lb fresh mussels, scrubbed
450g/1lb clams, scrubbed
4 cooked king prawns (jumbo shrimp) or
    scampi, in the shell
salt and ground black pepper
chopped fresh parsley and lemon wedges,
    to garnish

1 Heat the olive oil in a paella pan or large frying pan, add the onion and garlic and fry until translucent. Add the chorizo and fry until lightly golden.

2 Cut the bodies of the squids into rings and the tentacles into pieces. Add the squid to the pan and sauté over a high heat for 2 minutes.

3 Stir in the pepper and tomatoes and simmer gently for 5 minutes, until the pepper is tender. Pour in the stock and wine, stir well and bring to the boil. Stir in the rice and saffron and season well. Bring the liquid back to the boil, then lower the heat and simmer for about 10 minutes.

4 Gently stir the peas, prawns or scampi, mussels and clams into the rice, then cook for a further 15–20 minutes, until the rice is tender and all the mussels and clams have opened. (Discard any that remain closed.)

5 Remove the pan from the heat and arrange the king prawns or scampi on top. Cover and leave to stand for 5 minutes. Sprinkle the paella with chopped parsley and serve from the pan, accompanied by lemon wedges.

Nutritional information per portion: Energy 585kcal/2445kJ; Protein 36.1g; Carbohydrate 60.9g, of which sugars 10.1g; Fat 20.4g, of which saturates 5.6g; Cholesterol 268mg; Calcium 132mg; Fibre 4.2g; Sodium 1055mg.

Calderete of rice with fish and aioli

Cooking rice in fish stock gives it such a splendid flavour that it is often eaten on its own, served in a little cauldron and accompanied by aioli, with the fish to follow. If you prefer, the fish can be returned to the pan while the dish is still liquid, and the fish and rice eaten with the sauce.

SERVES 6

1.6kg/3½lb mixed fish on the bone, such
    as snapper, bream, grey or red mullet,
    or bass
45ml/3 tbsp olive oil
6 garlic cloves, smashed
1 *ñora* chilli or 1 hot dried chilli, seeded
    and chopped
250g/9oz ripe tomatoes, peeled, seeded
    and chopped
pinch of saffron threads (0.25g)
30ml/2 tbsp dry vermouth or white wine
1 tomato, finely diced
30ml/2 tbsp chopped fresh parsley
400g/14oz/2 cups paella rice, washed
115g/4oz small unshelled shrimps
salt and ground black pepper

FOR THE STOCK
1 onion, chopped
2 garlic cloves, chopped
1 celery stick, chopped
1 carrot, chopped
1 litre/1¾ pints/4 cups water

FOR THE AIOLI
4 garlic cloves, finely chopped
2.5ml/½ tsp salt
5ml/1 tsp lemon juice
2 egg yolks
250ml/8fl oz/1 cup olive oil

1 Remove the heads from the fish. Working from the head end, cut the skin along the top of the back and work the fillets off the bone. Trim as needed, put the fillets on a plate and salt them lightly. Cover and place in the refrigerator until required.

2 Make the fish stock. Put the bones, heads, tails and any other remaining bits into a large pan with the onion, garlic, celery, carrot and water. Bring to the boil, then reduce the heat, cover and simmer for about 30 minutes.

3 Make the aioli. Put the garlic in a large mortar with the salt and lemon juice and reduce to a purée. Add the egg yolks and mix thoroughly. Gradually work in the oil, drop by drop at first, to make a thick, mayonnaise-like sauce.

4 Put 15ml/1 tbsp of the olive oil in a small pan and add the whole smashed garlic cloves and dried chilli pieces. Fry for a few minutes until the garlic looks roasted.

5 Add the chopped tomatoes halfway through, crumble in the saffron and cook to form a sauce. Pour the sauce into a small blender and purée until smooth.

6 Heat the remaining 30ml/2 tbsp oil in a large frying pan and fry the fish pieces until they begin to stiffen. Strain the fish stock into a jug (pitcher), then add 900ml/1½ pints/3¾ cups stock and the tomato sauce to the fish. Cook the fish gently for a further 3–4 minutes, until slightly underdone.

7 Remove the fish pieces from the pan with a slotted spoon to a serving dish. Season lightly and sprinkle with the vermouth or wine, diced tomato and parsley. Cover with foil and keep warm.

8 Add the rice to the stock, stir, season and bring to a simmer. Cook for 18–20 minutes. Before all the liquid is absorbed, stir in the shrimps. When the rice is tender, cover and turn off the heat. Stand until all the liquid is absorbed: about 5 minutes. Serve from the pan, accompanied by the aioli. When the rice course is almost finished, uncover the fish. Stir the fish juices into the remains of the aioli, then pour over the fish. Eat on the same plates as the rice.

Nutritional information per portion: Energy 720kcal/2996kJ; Protein 31.3g; Carbohydrate 55g, of which sugars 1.8g; Fat 40.8g, of which saturates 5.6g; Cholesterol 136mg; Calcium 133mg; Fibre 0.6g; Sodium 873mg.

Vegetable rice pot

In this arroz de verduras, *fresh seasonal vegetables are cooked in slightly spiced rice. Always taste stock, and reduce it if necessary, before adding it to rice: this is your chance to change it.*

SERVES 4

1 large aubergine (eggplant)
45ml/3 tbsp olive oil
2 onions, quartered and sliced
2 garlic cloves, finely chopped
1 red (bell) pepper, halved, seeded and
   sliced
1 yellow (bell) pepper, halved, seeded and
   sliced
200g/7oz fine green beans, halved
115g/4oz/1½ cups brown cap (cremini)
   mushrooms, halved
300g/11oz/1½ cups paella rice, washed
   and drained
1 dried chilli, seeded and crumbled
1 litre/1¾ pints/4 cups chicken stock
115g/4oz/1 cup peas
60ml/4 tbsp chopped fresh parsley
salt and ground black pepper
fresh parsley or coriander (cilantro)
   leaves, to garnish

1 Halve the aubergine lengthways, then cut it into slices. Spread slices out in a large colander or on a draining board, sprinkle with salt and leave for about 30 minutes. Rinse under cold running water and pat dry with kitchen paper.

2 Heat 30ml/2 tbsp olive oil in a deep, wide frying pan or sauté pan over a high heat. Add the aubergine slices and sauté until golden, stirring occasionally, then transfer to kitchen paper to drain.

3 Add the remaining oil to the pan and cook the onion, and garlic until soft. Add the peppers, green beans and mushrooms and cook briefly. Add the drained rice and stir for 1–2 minutes, then stir in the aubergine. Add the chilli and seasoning. Add the stock. Add the peas and parsley and mix together.

4 Bring the mixture up to boiling point, then cover and cook over a low heat, for 20–25 minutes, checking the liquid level towards the end (the rice should absorb the liquid, but not burn). When the rice is tender, turn off the heat, cover the pan and leave to stand for 10 minutes for the remaining liquid to be absorbed. Garnish with the parsley or coriander and serve immediately.

Nutritional information per portion: Energy 454kcal/1891kJ; Protein 11.8g; Carbohydrate 78.3g, of which sugars 13.2g; Fat 10.4g, of which saturates 1.5g; Cholesterol 0mg; Calcium 98mg; Fibre 7.4g; Sodium 13mg.

Cuban-style rice

Arroz a la cubana, *garnished with fried eggs and bananas, is popular in the Canary Islands and Catalonia. It makes an easy and substantial supper dish.*

SERVES 4

3 garlic cloves
120ml/4fl oz/$^{1}/_{2}$ cup olive oil
300g/11oz/1$^{1}/_{2}$ cups long grain rice
15g/$^{1}/_{2}$oz/1 tbsp butter
4 small bananas or 2 large bananas
4 large (US extra large) eggs
salt and paprika

FOR THE TOMATO SAUCE

30ml/2 tbsp olive oil
1 onion, chopped
2 garlic cloves, finely chopped
800g/1lb 12oz can tomatoes
4 thyme or oregano sprigs
ground black pepper

1 Make the tomato sauce. Heat the oil in a pan, add the onion and garlic and fry gently, stirring, until soft. Stir in the tomatoes and thyme or oregano and simmer for 5 minutes. Add the seasoning. Remove the herbs and keep warm.

2 Put 850ml/1 pint 8fl oz/3$^{1}/_{2}$ cups water in a pan with two whole garlic cloves and 15ml/1 tbsp oil. Bring to the boil, add the rice and cook for 18 minutes until it is done, and the liquid has been absorbed.

3 Heat a pan with 30ml/2 tbsp oil and gently fry one chopped garlic clove. Add the rice, stir, season well, then turn off the heat and cover the pan.

4 Heat the butter in a frying pan with 15ml/1 tbsp oil. Halve the bananas lengthways and fry briefly on both sides. Keep them warm.

5 Add 60ml/4 tbsp oil to the pan and fry the eggs over a medium-high heat, until the edges turn golden. Season to taste with salt and paprika. Serve the rice surrounded by the tomato sauce, bananas and fried eggs.

Nutritional information per portion: Energy 668kcal/2781kJ; Protein 13.9g; Carbohydrate 76.6g, of which sugars 15.4g; Fat 34g, of which saturates 7.2g; Cholesterol 198mg; Calcium 64mg; Fibre 2.7g; Sodium 112mg.

Andrajos

This is a rich dish of hare, wine and mushrooms, flavoured with herbs and pine nuts. The name means "rags and tatters"; it was a shepherds' dish and the shepherd would have made his own simple flour and water pasta, cut into squares.

SERVES 6

800g/1¾lb hare meat and bone (the front legs and rib end)
200ml/7fl oz/scant 1 cup red wine
120–150ml/4–5fl oz/½–⅔ cup olive oil
150g/5oz bacon lardons, or diced pancetta
2 onions, chopped
2 large garlic cloves, finely chopped
8 baby onions, peeled
4 carrots, diced
4 chicken thighs, halved along the bone and seasoned

seasoned plain (all-purpose) flour, for dusting
350g/12oz small open-cap mushrooms
600ml/1 pint/2½ cups stock
5ml/1 tsp dried thyme
1 bay leaf
250g/9oz dried lasagne sheets
90ml/6 tbsp chopped fresh parsley
30ml/2 tbsp pine nuts
salt and ground black pepper

1 Starting at least two days ahead, cut the hare into portions and put in a bowl. Pour over the red wine and 15ml/1 tbsp of the oil and leave to marinate in the refrigerator for at least 24 hours.

2 Heat 30ml/2 tbsp olive oil in a large, heavy pan, add the bacon or pancetta, chopped onions and garlic and fry until the onions are translucent. Halfway through add the whole baby onions and diced carrots, and continue cooking, stirring occasionally.

3 Heat 45ml/3 tbsp oil in a large frying pan and fry the seasoned chicken pieces on both sides until golden brown. Add to the onion mixture.

4 Remove the hare from the red wine marinade, reserving the liquid. Blot the meat well on kitchen paper and dredge with the seasoned flour until well coated. Add more oil to the frying pan, if necessary, and fry the meat on all sides until browned.

5 Meanwhile, reserve eight of the smallest open-cap mushrooms. Quarter the remaining mushrooms and add to the chicken mixture. Continue cooking the hare in the frying pan, stirring every now and then, until browned.

6 When the hare is ready, arrange the pieces in the pan. Pour the reserved marinade into the frying pan to deglaze it, then pour the juices into the pan.

7 Add the stock, dried thyme and bay leaf and season with salt and pepper. Cook over a low heat for 1^1/$_2$ hours, until the meat is tender. Leave to cool.

8 When ready to serve, bring plenty of water to the boil in a large roasting pan with 5ml/1 tsp salt and 15ml/1 tbsp oil. Break up the lasagne sheets and spread out the pieces in the pan. Cook for 7–8 minutes until soft, moving the pieces around to prevent them from sticking.

9 Remove all the meat from the bones and return to the pan with 60ml/4 tbsp of the parsley. Bring to a simmer. Stir the drained pasta into the sauce. Heat 15ml/1 tbsp oil in a small pan and fry the reserved mushrooms, then arrange them on top. Sprinkle with the remaining parsley and the pine nuts, and serve.

Nutritional information per portion: Energy 589kcal/2464kJ; Protein 42.4g; Carbohydrate 38g, of which sugars 7g; Fat 28.3g, of which saturates 6.2g; Cholesterol 152mg; Calcium 75mg; Fibre 3.5g; Sodium 430mg.

San Esteban canelones

Catalans are fond of pasta, and canelones *are traditional on* San Esteban, *the day after Christmas Day. Try to keep all the chopped stuffing ingredients the same size – small dice.*

SERVES 4–8

60ml/4 tbsp olive oil
1 onion, finely chopped
1 carrot, finely chopped
2 garlic cloves, finely chopped
2 ripe tomatoes, peeled and
    finely chopped
25g/1oz/2 tbsp butter
150g/5oz raw chicken livers or
    cooked stuffing, diced
150g/5oz raw pork or cooked ham,
    gammon or sausage, diced
250g/9oz raw or cooked chicken, diced
5ml/1 tsp fresh thyme leaves
30ml/2 tbsp brandy

90ml/6 tbsp crème fraîche or double
    (heavy) cream
16 no pre-cook cannelloni tubes
75g/3oz/1 cup freshly grated Parmesan
    cheese
salt and ground black pepper
green salad, to serve

FOR THE WHITE SAUCE
50g/2oz/¼ cup butter
50g/2oz/½ cup plain (all-purpose) flour
900ml/1½ pints/3¾ cups milk
freshly grated nutmeg, to taste

1 Heat the oil in a large frying pan, add the onion, carrot, garlic and tomatoes and cook over a low heat, stirring, for about 10 minutes or until very soft.

2 Add the butter, then the raw meat, to the pan and cook until coloured. Add the remaining meats and sprinkle first with thyme, then with the brandy. Stir, then warm through and reduce the liquid.

3 Pour in the crème fraîche or cream, season to taste and leave to simmer for about 10 minutes. Cool briefly.

4 Preheat the oven to 190°C/375°F/Gas 5. Melt the butter in a pan, add the flour and cook, stirring, for 1–2 minutes. Gradually stir in the milk, a little at a time. Bring to simmering point, stirring until the sauce is smooth. Grate in nutmeg to taste, then season with plenty of salt and black pepper.

5 Spoon a little of the white sauce into a baking dish. Fill the cannelloni tubes with the meat mixture and arrange in a single layer in the dish. Pour the remaining white sauce over them, then sprinkle with the Parmesan cheese. Bake in the oven for 35–40 minutes, or until the pasta is tender. Leave for 10 minutes before serving with green salad.

Nutritional information per portion: Energy 480kcal/2014kJ; Protein 27.4g; Carbohydrate 40.5g, of which sugars 8.9g; Fat 23.5g, of which saturates 11.4g; Cholesterol 148mg; Calcium 282mg; Fibre 1.9g; Sodium 473mg.

Fish and shellfish

Fish and shellfish are one of the glories

of Spanish cooking, largely because Spain

is bordered by the Mediterranean and the

Atlantic and has some of the best fishing

in the world. In this chapter, you'll find

a selection of appetizers, salads and main

courses, including whole baked fish in

simple sauces and chargrilled squid.

Seafood salad

Ensalada de Mariscos *is a very pretty arrangement of fresh mussels, prawns and squid rings served on a colourful bed of salad vegetables. In Spain, canned albacore tuna is also often included in this type of simple salad.*

SERVES 6

115g/4oz prepared squid rings
12 fresh mussels, scrubbed and beards
   removed
1 large carrot
6 crisp lettuce leaves
10cm/4in piece cucumber, finely diced
115g/4oz cooked, peeled prawns (shrimp)
15ml/1 tbsp drained pickled capers

FOR THE DRESSING
30ml/2 tbsp freshly squeezed lemon juice
45ml/3 tbsp extra virgin olive oil
15ml/1 tbsp chopped fresh parsley
salt and ground black pepper

1 Put the squid rings into a metal sieve or vegetable steamer. Place the sieve or steamer over a pan of simmering water, cover with a lid and steam the squid for 2–3 minutes until it just turns white. Cool quickly under cold running water to prevent further cooking and drain thoroughly on kitchen paper.

2 Discard any open mussels that do not close when tapped. Cover the base of a large pan with water, add the mussels, then cover and steam for a few minutes until they open. Discard any that remain shut. Leave to cool.

3 Using a swivel-style vegetable peeler, cut the carrot into wafer-thin ribbons. Tear the lettuce into pieces and arrange on a serving plate. Add the carrot ribbons on top of the lettuce, then sprinkle over the diced cucumber.

4 Arrange the mussels, prawns and squid rings over the salad and sprinkle the capers over the top.

5 Make the dressing. Put all the ingredients in a bowl and whisk well to combine. Drizzle over the salad. Serve at room temperature.

Nutritional information per portion: Energy 100kcal/415kJ; Protein 8.1g; Carbohydrate 2.6g, of which sugars 2g; Fat 6.4g, of which saturates 1g; Cholesterol 85mg; Calcium 50mg; Fibre 1.1g; Sodium 95mg.

Potato, mussel and watercress salad

The mussels found on the Galician coast are the best in the world. The Galicians are also very proud of their potatoes and their watercress. In ensalada de mejillones, patatas y berros *a creamy, well-flavoured dressing enhances all these ingredients.*

SERVES 4

675g/1½lb salad potatoes
1kg/2¼lb mussels, scrubbed and beards removed
200ml/7fl oz/scant 1 cup dry white wine
15g/½oz fresh flat leaf parsley, chopped
1 bunch of watercress or rocket (arugula)
salt and ground black pepper
chopped fresh chives or spring onion (scallion) tops, to garnish

FOR THE DRESSING

105ml/7 tbsp olive oil
15–30ml/1–2 tbsp white wine vinegar
5ml/1 tsp strong Dijon mustard
1 large shallot, very finely chopped
15ml/1 tbsp chopped fresh chives
45ml/3 tbsp double (heavy) cream
pinch of caster (superfine) sugar (optional)

1 Cook the potatoes in salted boiling water for 15–20 minutes, or until tender. Drain, cool, then peel. Slice into a bowl and toss with 30ml/2 tbsp of the oil for the dressing.

2 Discard any open mussels. Bring the white wine to the boil in a large, heavy pan. Add the mussels, cover and boil vigorously, shaking the pan occasionally, for 3–4 minutes, until the mussels have opened. Discard any that do not open. Drain and shell the mussels, reserving the cooking liquid.

3 Boil the reserved mussel cooking liquid until reduced to about 45ml/3 tbsp. Strain through a fine sieve over the potatoes and toss to mix.

4 To make the dressing, whisk together the remaining oil, 15ml/1 tbsp of the vinegar, the mustard, shallot and chives. Add the cream and whisk again. Adjust the seasoning, adding a little more vinegar and/or sugar to taste.

5 Toss the mussels with the potatoes, then mix in the dressing and chopped parsley. Arrange the watercress or rocket on a serving platter and top with the salad. Serve sprinkled with extra chives or a little spring onion.

Nutritional information per portion: Energy 459kcal/1918kJ; Protein 17.2g; Carbohydrate 29.2g, of which sugars 3.8g; Fat 27.7g, of which saturates 7g; Cholesterol 45mg; Calcium 222mg; Fibre 2.5g; Sodium 231mg.

Surtido de pescado

The Spanish enjoy and make the most of preserved fish. This is a very pretty dish, which uses whatever fish is available at the time, and is an ideal last-minute party appetizer.

SERVES 4

6 eggs
cos or romaine lettuce leaves
75–90ml/5–6 tbsp mayonnaise
90g/3¹/₂oz jar Avruga herring roe,
    Eurocaviar grey mullet roe or undyed
    (or black) lumpfish roe
2 x 115g/4oz cans sardines in oil
2 x 115g/4oz cans mackerel fillets in oil
2 x 150g/5oz jars cockles (small clams) in
    brine, drained
2 x 115g/4oz cans mussels or scallops in
    tomato sauce
fresh flat leaf parsley or dill sprigs,
    to garnish

1 Put the eggs in a pan with enough water to cover and bring to the boil. Turn down the heat and simmer for 10 minutes. Drain, then cover with cold water and set aside until completely cool. Peel the eggs and slice in half.

2 Arrange the lettuce leaves on a large serving platter, with the tips pointing outwards. (You may need to break off the bottom end of each leaf if the leaves are large.)

3 Place a teaspoonful or so of mayonnaise on the flat side of each halved egg and top with a spoonful of fish caviar. Carefully arrange in the centre of the dish.

4 Arrange the sardines and mackerel fillets at four points on the plate. Spoon the pickled cockles into two of the gaps, opposite each other, and the mussels in sauce in the remaining gaps. Garnish with parsley sprigs or dill. Chill until needed.

Nutritional information per portion: Energy 622kcal/2588kJ; Protein 56.1g; Carbohydrate 2.7g, of which sugars 0.7g; Fat 43.2g, of which saturates 8.8g; Cholesterol 482mg; Calcium 373mg; Fibre 0.2g; Sodium 661mg.

Fried whitebait with sherry salsa

Small freshly fried fish are good for a tasty starter or a snack. Black-backed anchovies are the best, but need to be cooked within a day of catching. Serve the fish with lemon wedges.

SERVES 4

225g/8oz whitebait
30ml/2 tbsp seasoned plain
   (all-purpose) flour
60ml/4 tbsp olive oil
60ml/4 tbsp sunflower oil

FOR THE SALSA
1 shallot, finely chopped
2 garlic cloves, finely chopped
4 ripe tomatoes, roughly chopped
1 small red chilli, seeded and chopped
30ml/2 tbsp olive oil
60ml/4 tbsp sweet oloroso sherry
30–45ml/2–3 tbsp chopped mixed fresh
   herbs, such as parsley or basil
25g/1oz/½ cup stale white breadcrumbs
salt and ground black pepper

1 To make the salsa, place the chopped shallot, garlic, tomatoes, chilli and olive oil in a pan. Cover with a lid and cook gently for about 10 minutes.

2 Pour the sherry into the pan and season with the salt and black pepper to taste. Stir in the herbs and breadcrumbs, then cover and keep the salsa hot until the whitebait are ready.

3 Preheat the oven to 150°C/300°F/Gas 2. Wash the whitebait thoroughly, drain well and dry on kitchen paper, then dust in the seasoned flour.

4 Heat the oils together in a heavy frying pan and cook the fish in batches until crisp and golden. Drain on kitchen paper and keep warm until all the fish are cooked. Serve at once with the salsa.

Nutritional information per portion: Energy 407kcal/1689kJ; Protein 13g; Carbohydrate 13.1g, of which sugars 5.1g; Fat 32.8g, of which saturates 3.4g; Cholesterol 0mg; Calcium 526mg; Fibre 2g; Sodium 191mg.

Salt cod fritters with aioli

Bacalao – salt cod – is one of the great Spanish delights, adding flavour to bland ingredients such as potatoes. If you are unfamiliar with it, then this is a delightful way to try it out. Bitesize fish cakes, dipped into rich, creamy, garlicky aioli, are irresistible as a tapas dish or appetizer.

SERVES 6

450g/1lb salt cod
500g/1¼lb floury potatoes
300ml/½ pint/1¼ cups milk
6 spring onions (scallions),
    finely chopped
30ml/2 tbsp extra virgin olive oil
30ml/2 tbsp chopped fresh parsley
juice of ½ lemon
2 eggs, beaten
plain (all-purpose) flour, for dusting
90g/3½oz/1¼ cups dried white
    breadcrumbs

olive oil, for shallow frying
salt and ground black pepper
lemon wedges and salad leaves, to serve

FOR THE AIOLI

2 large garlic cloves, finely chopped
2 egg yolks
300ml/½ pint/1¼ cups olive oil
juice of ½ lemon, to taste

1 Soak the salt cod in cold water for at least 24 hours, changing the water two or three times. The cod should swell as it rehydrates. Sample a tiny piece. It should not taste unpleasantly salty when fully rehydrated. Drain well and pat dry with kitchen paper.

2 Cook the potatoes, unpeeled, in a pan of lightly salted boiling water for about 20 minutes, until tender. Drain. As soon as they are cool enough to handle, peel the potatoes, then mash with a fork or use a potato masher.

3 Pour the milk into a pan, add half the spring onions and simmer. Add the soaked cod and poach gently for 10–15 minutes, until it flakes easily. Remove the cod and flake it with a fork into a bowl, discarding bones and skin.

4 Add 60ml/4 tbsp mashed potato to the cod and beat them together with a wooden spoon. Work in the olive oil, then gradually add the remaining mashed potato. Beat in the remaining spring onions and the parsley.

5 Season with lemon juice and pepper to taste – the mixture may also need a little salt but taste it before adding any. Add one beaten egg to the mixture and beat in until thoroughly combined, then chill until firm.

6 Shape the chilled fish mixture into 12–18 balls, then gently flatten into small round cakes. Coat each one in flour, then dip in the remaining beaten egg and coat with dried breadcrumbs. Chill until ready to fry.

7 Meanwhile, make the aioli. Place the garlic and a good pinch of salt in a mortar and pound to a paste with a pestle. Using a small whisk or a wooden spoon, gradually work in the egg yolks.

8 Beat in about half the olive oil, a drop at a time. When the sauce is as thick as soft butter, beat in 5–10ml/1–2 tsp lemon juice. Continue adding oil until the aioli is very thick. Season to taste, adding more lemon juice if you wish.

9 Heat about 2cm/¾in oil in a large frying pan. Add the fritters and cook over a medium-high heat for about 4 minutes. Turn them over and cook for a further 4 minutes on the other side, until crisp and golden. Drain on kitchen paper, then serve with the aioli, lemon wedges and salad leaves.

Nutritional information per portion: Energy 653kcal/2721kJ; Protein 32.7g; Carbohydrate 28.1g, of which sugars 4.2g; Fat 46.4g, of which saturates 7.6g; Cholesterol 178mg; Calcium 123mg; Fibre 1.4g; Sodium 472mg.

Sardines en escabeche

The Arabs invented marinades as a means of preserving meat, and escabeche *means "acid" in Arabic. The fish are always fried first and then stored in vinegar.*

SERVES 2–4

12–16 sardines, cleaned
seasoned plain (all-purpose) flour
30ml/2 tbsp olive oil
roasted red onion, green (bell) pepper
    and tomatoes, to garnish

FOR THE MARINADE
90ml/6 tbsp olive oil
1 onion, sliced
1 garlic clove, crushed
3–4 bay leaves
2 cloves
1 dried red chilli, seeded and chopped
5ml/1 tsp paprika
120ml/4fl oz/1/2 cup wine vinegar or
    sherry vinegar
120ml/4fl oz/1/2 cup white wine
salt and ground black pepper

1 Using a sharp knife, cut the heads off the sardines and split each of them along the belly. Turn the fish over so that the backbone is uppermost. Press down along the backbone to loosen it, then carefully lift out the backbone and as many of the remaining little bones as possible. Close the sardines up and dust them with the flour.

2 Heat the olive oil in a frying pan and fry the sardines for 2–3 minutes on each side. With a metal spatula, remove the fish to a plate and allow to cool, then pack them in a single layer in a large, shallow non-metallic dish.

3 To make the marinade, add the olive oil to the oil remaining in the frying pan. Fry the onion and garlic gently for 5–10 minutes until soft and translucent, stirring occasionally. Add the bay leaves, cloves, chilli and paprika, with pepper to taste. Fry, stirring frequently, for another 1–2 minutes.

4 Stir in the vinegar, wine and a little salt. Allow to bubble up, then pour over the sardines. The marinade should cover the fish completely. When the fish is cool, cover and chill overnight or for up to three days. Serve the sardines and their marinade, garnished with the onion, pepper and tomatoes.

Nutritional information per portion: Energy 242kcal/1004kJ; Protein 15.8g; Carbohydrate 1.7g, of which sugars 0.9g; Fat 18.1g, of which saturates 3.6g; Cholesterol 0mg; Calcium 70mg; Fibre 0.2g; Sodium 92mg.

Truchas a la Navarra

Traditionally, the trout would have come from mountain streams and been stuffed and wrapped in locally cured ham. One of the beauties of this method is that the skins come off in one piece.

SERVES 4

4 brown or rainbow trout, about 250g/9oz each, cleaned
16 thin slices Serrano ham, about 200g/7oz
50g/2oz/¼ cup melted butter, plus extra for greasing
salt and ground black pepper
buttered potatoes, to serve (optional)

1 Extend the belly cavity of each trout, cutting up one side of the backbone. Slip a knife behind the rib bones to loosen them (sometimes just flexing the fish makes them pop up). Snip these off from both sides with scissors, and season the fish well inside.

2 Preheat the grill (broiler) to high, with a shelf in the top position. Line a baking tray with foil and butter it.

3 Working with the fish on the foil, fold a piece of ham into each belly. Use smaller or broken bits of ham for this, and reserve the eight best slices.

4 Brush each trout with a little butter, seasoning the outside lightly with salt and pepper. Wrap two ham slices round each one, crossways, tucking the ends into the belly. Grill (broil) the trout for 4 minutes, then carefully turn them over with a metal spatula, rolling them across on the belly, so the ham doesn't come loose, and grill for a further 4 minutes.

5 Serve the trout very hot, with any spare butter spooned over the top. Diners should open the trout on their plates, and eat them from the inside.

Nutritional information per portion: Energy 369kcal/1546kJ; Protein 48g; Carbohydrate 0.6g, of which sugars 0.6g; Fat 19.4g, of which saturates 8.8g; Cholesterol 216mg; Calcium 66mg; Fibre 0g; Sodium 821mg.

Baked trout with rice, tomatoes and nuts

Trout is very popular in Spain, particularly in the north. Here is a modern recipe for trucha rellena, *baked in foil with a rice stuffing in which sun-dried tomatoes are used instead of chillies.*

SERVES 4

2 trout, about 500g/1¼lb each
75g/3oz/¾ cup mixed unsalted almonds, pine nuts or hazelnuts
25ml/1½ tbsp olive oil, plus extra for drizzling
1 small onion, finely chopped
10ml/2 tsp grated fresh root ginger
175g/6oz/1½ cups cooked white long grain rice
4 tomatoes, peeled and very finely chopped
4 sun-dried tomatoes in oil, drained and chopped
30ml/2 tbsp chopped fresh tarragon
2 fresh tarragon sprigs
salt and ground black pepper
dressed green salad leaves, to serve

1 Preheat the oven to 190°C/375°F/Gas 5. If the trout is unfilleted, use a sharp knife to fillet it. Remove any tiny bones remaining in the cavity using a pair of tweezers.

2 Spread out the nuts in a baking tray and bake for 3–4 minutes until golden brown, shaking the tray occasionally. Chop the nuts roughly.

3 Heat the olive oil in a small frying pan and fry the onion for 3–4 minutes until soft and translucent. Stir in the grated ginger, cook for a further 1 minute, then spoon into a mixing bowl. Stir the rice, chopped and sun-dried tomatoes, toasted nuts and tarragon into the onion mixture. Season well.

4 Place the trout on individual large pieces of oiled foil and spoon the stuffing into the cavities. Add a sprig of tarragon and a drizzle of olive oil or oil from the sun-dried tomatoes.

5 Fold the foil over to enclose each trout completely, and put the parcels in a large roasting pan. Bake for about 20 minutes or until the fish is just tender. Cut the fish into thick slices. Serve with the salad leaves.

Nutritional information per portion: Energy 458kcal/1920kJ; Protein 45.1g; Carbohydrate 19.4g, of which sugars 5g; Fat 22.8g, of which saturates 3.4g; Cholesterol 160mg; Calcium 146mg; Fibre 3.2g; Sodium 161mg.

Grilled red mullet with bay leaves

Red mullet are called salmonetes – *little salmon – in Spain because of their delicate, pale pink colour. They are simple to cook on a barbecue, with bay leaves and a dribble of tangy dressing.*

SERVES 4

4 red mullet, about 225–275g/8–10oz
each, cleaned and descaled if cooking
under a grill (broiler)
olive oil, for brushing
fresh herb sprigs, such as fennel, dill,
parsley, or thyme
2–3 dozen fresh or dried bay leaves

FOR THE DRESSING
90ml/6 tbsp olive oil
6 garlic cloves, finely chopped
1/2 dried chilli, seeded and chopped
juice of 1/2 lemon
15ml/1 tbsp parsley

1 Prepare the barbecue or preheat the grill (broiler) with the shelf 15cm/6in from the heat source.

2 Brush each fish with oil and stuff the cavities with the herb sprigs. Brush the grill pan with oil and lay bay leaves across the cooking rack. Place the fish on top of the leaves and cook for 15–20 minutes until cooked through, turning once.

3 To make the dressing, heat the olive oil in a small pan and fry the chopped garlic with the dried chilli. Add the lemon juice and strain the dressing into a small jug (pitcher). Add the chopped parsley and stir to combine.

4 Place the mullet on warmed plates, drizzled with the dressing, and serve.

Nutritional information per portion: Energy 295kcal/1226kJ; Protein 24.3g; Carbohydrate 0.5g, of which sugars 0.1g; Fat 21.8g, of which saturates 2.4g; Cholesterol 0mg; Calcium 98mg; Fibre 0.3g; Sodium 126mg.

Mackerel in samfaina

Samfaina is a sauce from the east coast of Spain and the Costa Brava. It is rather like a chunky vegetable stew and offsets the richness of the mackerel.

SERVES 4

2 large mackerel, filleted, or 4 fillets
plain (all-purpose) flour, for dusting
30ml/2 tbsp olive oil
lemon wedges, to serve

FOR THE SAMFAINA SAUCE
1 large aubergine (eggplant)
60ml/4 tbsp olive oil
1 large onion, chopped
2 garlic cloves, finely chopped
1 large courgette (zucchini), sliced
1 red and 1 green (bell) pepper, seeded
  and cut into squares
800g/1¾lb ripe tomatoes, chopped
1 bay leaf
salt and ground black pepper

1 Make the sauce. Peel the aubergine, then cut the flesh into cubes, sprinkle with salt and leave to stand in a colander for 30 minutes.

2 Heat half the oil in large, heavy pan. Fry the onion over a medium heat until it colours. Add the garlic, then the courgette and peppers and stir-fry. Add the tomatoes and bay leaf, partially cover and simmer over the lowest heat, letting the tomatoes just soften.

3 Rinse off the salt from the aubergine. Using three layers of kitchen paper, squeeze the aubergine cubes dry. Heat the remaining oil in a frying pan until smoking. Add the aubergine cubes a handful at a time, stirring and cooking over a high heat until brown all over. Stir into the tomato sauce.

4 Cut each mackerel into three pieces, and dust the filleted side with flour. Heat the oil in a frying pan over a high heat and put the fish in, floured side down. Fry for 3 minutes until golden. Turn and cook for another 1 minute, then slip the fish into the sauce and simmer, covered, for 5 minutes. Adjust the seasonings before serving.

Nutritional information per portion: Energy 621kcal/2591kJ; Protein 34.3g; Carbohydrate 32.4g, of which sugars 29.4g; Fat 40.6g, of which saturates 7.6g; Cholesterol 66mg; Calcium 134mg; Fibre 19.4g; Sodium 111mg.

Fried sole with lemon and capers

Flat fish of different sorts abound in the Mediterranean and are usually fried simply and served with lemon wedges to squeeze over the top. Intensely flavoured capers, which grow extensively in the Balearic Islands, make a tangy addition.

SERVES 2

30–45ml/2–3 tbsp plain
  (all-purpose) flour
4 sole, plaice or flounder fillets,
  or 2 whole small flat fish
45ml/3 tbsp olive oil
25g/1oz/2 tbsp butter

60ml/4 tbsp lemon juice
30ml/2 tbsp pickled capers, drained
salt and ground black pepper
fresh flat leaf parsley, to garnish
lemon wedges, to serve

1 Sift the flour on to a plate and season well with salt and ground black pepper. Dip the fish fillets into the flour, to coat evenly on both sides.

2 Heat the oil and butter in a large frying pan until foaming. Add the fish fillets and fry over a medium heat for 2–3 minutes on each side.

3 Lift out the fillets carefully with a metal spatula and place them on a warmed serving platter. Season with salt and ground black pepper.

4 Add the lemon juice and capers to the pan, heat through and pour over the fish. Garnish with parsley, then serve with the lemon wedges.

COOK'S TIP
This is a flavourful, and quick, way to serve the fillets of any white fish. The delicate flavour is enhanced by the tangy lemon juice and capers.

Nutritional information per portion: Energy 425kcal/1773kJ; Protein 34.2g; Carbohydrate 5.9g, of which sugars 0.2g; Fat 29.7g, of which saturates 9.3g; Cholesterol 111mg; Calcium 103mg; Fibre 0.3g; Sodium 316mg.

Sea bass in a salt crust

Baking fish in a salt crust enhances the flavour and brings out the taste of the sea. In Spain, the gilt-head bream is the fish most often used, but any firm fish can be cooked in this way.

SERVES 4–6

1 sea bass, about 1kg/2¼lb, gutted
   and scaled
1 sprig each of fresh fennel, rosemary
   and thyme
mixed peppercorns
2kg/4½lb coarse sea salt
seaweed or samphire, to garnish
   (optional)
lemon slices, to serve

1 Preheat the oven to 240°C/ 475°F/Gas 9. Fill the cavity of the sea bass with the fennel, rosemary and thyme and grind over some of the mixed peppercorns.

2 Spread half the salt in a shallow baking tray and lay the sea bass on it.

3 Cover the fish all over with a 1cm/½in layer of salt, pressing it down firmly. Bake for 30 minutes, until the salt coagulates and is beginning to colour.

4 To serve, leave the fish on the baking tray and garnish with seaweed or samphire, if using. Bring the fish to the table in its salt crust. Use a sharp knife to break open the crust so that the glorious aromas are released.

Nutritional information per portion: Energy 117kcal/491kJ; Protein 22.5g; Carbohydrate 0g, of which sugars 0g; Fat 2.9g, of which saturates 0.5g; Cholesterol 93mg; Calcium 152mg; Fibre 0g; Sodium 736mg.

Monkfish with pimiento and cream sauce

This recipe comes from Rioja country, where a special horned red pepper is used to make a spicy sauce. Here, red peppers are used with a little chilli while cream makes a mellow pink sauce.

SERVES 4

2 large red (bell) peppers

1kg/2¼lb monkfish tail or 900g/2lb halibut

plain (all-purpose) flour, for dusting

30ml/2 tbsp olive oil

25g/1oz/2 tbsp butter

120ml/4fl oz/½ cup white Rioja or dry vermouth

½ dried chilli, seeded and chopped

8 raw prawns (shrimp), in the shell

150ml/¼ pint/⅔ cup double (heavy) cream

salt and ground black pepper

fresh flat leaf parsley, to garnish

1 Preheat the grill (broiler) to high and cook the peppers for 8–12 minutes, turning occasionally, until they are soft, and the skins blackened. Leave to cool slightly. Skin and discard the stalks and seeds. Put the flesh into a blender, strain in the juices and purée.

2 Cut the fish into 8 steaks. Season well and dust with flour.

3 Heat the oil and butter in a frying pan and fry the fish for 3 minutes on each side. Lift out and keep warm.

4 Add the wine or vermouth and chilli to the pan and stir to deglaze the pan. Add the prawns and cook briefly, then lift out and reserve.

5 Boil the sauce to reduce by half, then strain into a small jug (pitcher). Add the cream to the pan and boil briefly to reduce.

6 Return the sauce to the pan, stir in the peppers and adjust seasoning. Pour the sauce over the fish and serve garnished with the cooked prawns and parsley.

Nutritional information per portion: Energy 500kcal/2087kJ; Protein 49.7g; Carbohydrate 7.2g, of which sugars 6.9g; Fat 27.1g, of which saturates 13.7g; Cholesterol 140mg; Calcium 70mg; Fibre 1.4g; Sodium 113mg.

Vieiras de Santiago

Scallops are the symbol of St James (Santiago), and this dish is associated with his shrine at Santiago de Compostela. The scallops are covered in tomato sauce and are served in the shell.

SERVES 4

30ml/2 tbsp olive oil
1 onion, finely chopped
2 garlic cloves, finely chopped
200g/7oz can tomatoes
pinch of cayenne pepper
45ml/3 tbsp finely chopped fresh parsley
50ml/2fl oz/¼ cup orange juice
50g/2oz/4 tbsp butter
450g/1lb large shelled scallops,
    or 8–12 large ones on the shell,
    detached and cleaned
30ml/2 tbsp anis spirit, such as Ricard
    or Pernod
90ml/6 tbsp stale breadcrumbs
salt and ground black pepper

1 Heat the oil in a pan and fry the onion and garlic over a gentle heat. Add the tomatoes and cook for 10–15 minutes, stirring occasionally. Season with a little salt and cayenne pepper. Transfer to a food processor or blender, add 30ml/2 tbsp of the parsley and the orange juice and blend to form a purée.

2 Preheat the grill (broiler) with the shelf at its highest. Arrange four curved scallop shells, or flameproof ramekin dishes, on a baking tray. Heat 25g/1oz/ 2 tbsp of the butter in a small frying pan and fry the scallops gently, for about 2 minutes, or until sealed but not totally cooked through.

3 Pour the anis into a ladle and set light to it. Pour over the scallops and shake the pan gently until the flames die down. Divide the scallops among the shells and salt them lightly. Add the pan juices to the tomato sauce.

4 Pour the tomato sauce over the scallops. Mix together the breadcrumbs and the remaining parsley, season very lightly and sprinkle over the top. Melt the remaining butter in a small pan and drizzle over the breadcrumbs. Grill (broil) the scallops for about 1 minute to heat through. Serve immediately.

Nutritional information per portion: Energy 394kcal/1652kJ; Protein 29.7g; Carbohydrate 25.5g, of which sugars 4.4g; Fat 18.1g, of which saturates 7.8g; Cholesterol 80mg; Calcium 95mg; Fibre 1.8g; Sodium 459mg.

Hake and clams with salsa verde

*Merluza en salsa verde **is a favourite Basque way of cooking hake. As they bake, the clams open up and add their delicious sea juices to the green wine and parsley sauce.***

SERVES 4

4 hake steaks, about 2cm/³/₄in thick
50g/2oz/¹/₂ cup plain (all-purpose) flour,
   for dusting, plus 30ml/2 tbsp
60ml/4 tbsp olive oil
15ml/1 tbsp lemon juice
1 small onion, finely chopped
4 garlic cloves, finely chopped
150ml/¹/₄ pint/²/₃ cup fish stock
150ml/¹/₄ pint/²/₃ cup white wine
90ml/6 tbsp chopped fresh parsley
75g/3oz/³/₄ cup frozen petits pois
16 fresh clams, cleaned
salt and ground black pepper

1 Preheat the oven to 180°C/350°F/Gas 4. Season the fish, then dust with flour. Heat half the oil in a large pan, add the fish and fry for 1 minute on each side. Transfer to an ovenproof dish and sprinkle with the lemon juice.

2 Heat the remaining oil in a clean pan and fry the onion and garlic, stirring, until soft. Stir in the 30ml/2 tbsp flour and cook for about 1 minute.

3 Slowly add the stock and wine to the pan, stirring until thickened. Add 75ml/5 tbsp of the parsley and the petits pois to the sauce and season with plenty of salt and pepper.

4 Pour the sauce over the fish, and bake for 15–20 minutes, adding the clams 3–4 minutes before the end of the cooking time.

5 Discard any clams that do not open once cooked, then sprinkle the fish with the remaining parsley and serve.

Nutritional information per portion: Energy 347kcal/1449kJ; Protein 34.2g; Carbohydrate 13.2g, of which sugars 1.4g; Fat 15.2g, of which saturates 2.2g; Cholesterol 51mg; Calcium 109mg; Fibre 2.4g; Sodium 460mg.

Marmitako

This is a traditional fisherman's stew, often made at sea, with meaty tuna steaks. The substantial fish is wonderfully balanced by sweet peppers and cider, all topped by potatoes. It takes its name from the cooking pot, known in France as a "marmite".

SERVES 4

60ml/4 tbsp olive oil

1 onion, chopped

2 garlic cloves, finely chopped

3 green (bell) peppers, seeded and
   chopped

1/2 dried hot chilli, seeded and chopped

4 light tuna or bonito steaks, about
   150g/5oz each

400g/14oz can tomatoes with juice

10ml/2 tsp paprika

3 potatoes, diced

350ml/12fl oz/1¹/₂ cups dry (hard) cider

salt and ground black pepper

30ml/2 tbsp chopped fresh parsley,
   to garnish

1 Heat half the oil in a heavy pan big enough to take the fish. Fry the onion gently until softened, then add the garlic. Add the chopped peppers and chilli and stir-fry gently.

2 Season the fish steaks. Heat the remaining oil in a frying pan and fry the fish steaks for 2 minutes on each side over a high heat. Add the tomatoes to the vegetables and stir-fry briefly. Add the paprika, then season with salt and pepper to taste.

3 Slip the fish steaks into the sauce, moving the peppers into the spaces between them. Cover with the potatoes, pushing them as flat as possible. Add the cider and bring to a simmer. Cover and cook very gently for about 45 minutes, or until the potatoes are done. Check the seasoning, sprinkle with the chopped parsley and serve immediately, straight from the pan.

Nutritional information per portion: Energy 457kcal/1919kJ; Protein 39.2g; Carbohydrate 28.2g, of which sugars 16.4g; Fat 19.1g, of which saturates 3.7g; Cholesterol 42mg; Calcium 58mg; Fibre 4.4g; Sodium 100mg.

Chargrilled squid

Calamares a la plancha *are traditionally cooked on the hot griddle that is an essential part of every Spanish kitchen. The method is fast and simple and brings out the flavour of the squid.*

SERVES 4

**2 whole cleaned squid, with tentacles,
    about 275g/10oz each**
75ml/5 tbsp olive oil
30ml/2 tbsp sherry vinegar
2 fresh red chillies, finely chopped
60ml/4 tbsp dry white wine
salt and ground black pepper
hot cooked rice, to serve
**15–30ml/1–2 tbsp chopped parsley,
    to garnish**

1 Make a cut down the side of the body of each squid, then open it out flat. Score the flesh on both sides of the bodies in a criss-cross pattern. Chop the tentacles into short lengths. Place all the pieces in a non-metallic dish.

2 Whisk together the oil and vinegar in a bowl. Add salt and pepper to taste, pour over the squid and toss to mix. Cover and leave to marinate for 1 hour.

3 Heat a ridged griddle pan until hot. Add the body of one of the squid and cook over a medium heat for 2–3 minutes, pressing the squid with a metal spatula to make sure it stays flat. Repeat on the other side. Cook the other squid body in the same way.

4 Cut the squid bodies into diagonal strips and arrange on the rice. Keep hot. Add the tentacles and chillies to the pan and toss over a medium heat for 2 minutes. Stir in the wine, then drizzle over the squid. Garnish with parsley.

Nutritional information per portion: Energy 258kcal/1076kJ; Protein 23.5g; Carbohydrate 2g, of which sugars 0.2g; Fat 16.4g, of which saturates 2.6g; Cholesterol 338mg; Calcium 25mg; Fibre 0g; Sodium 167mg.

Calamares rellenos

Squid are often just stuffed with their own tentacles but, in this recipe, ham and raisins, which contrast wonderfully with the subtle flavour of the squid, are also included.

SERVES 4

2 squid, about 275g/10oz each
60ml/4 tbsp olive oil
1 small onion, finely chopped
2 garlic cloves, finely chopped
50g/2oz Serrano ham or gammon steak, diced finely
75g/3oz/scant 1/2 cup long grain rice
30ml/2 tbsp raisins, chopped
30ml/2 tbsp finely chopped fresh parsley
1/2 small (US medium) egg, beaten
plain (all-purpose) flour, for dusting
250ml/8fl oz/1 cup white wine
1 bay leaf
30ml/2 tbsp chopped fresh parsley
salt, paprika and black pepper

FOR THE TOMATO SAUCE

30ml/2 tbsp olive oil
1 onion, finely chopped
2 garlic cloves, finely chopped
200g/7oz can tomatoes
salt and cayenne pepper

1 Make the tomato sauce. Heat the oil in a heavy pan large enough to hold the squid. Gently fry the onion and garlic. Add the tomatoes and cook for 10–15 minutes. Season with salt and cayenne pepper.

2 To prepare the squid, use the tentacles to pull out the body. Cut off the tentacles, discarding the eyes and everything below. Flex the bodies to pop out the spinal structure. Chop the fin flaps and rinse the bodies well.

3 Heat half the oil in a pan and gently fry the onion and garlic together. Add the ham and squid tentacles and stir-fry. Off the heat stir in the rice, chopped raisins and parsley. Season well and add the egg to bind the ingredients.

4 Spoon the mixture into the squid bodies, then stitch each of them shut using a small skewer. Blot them with kitchen paper, then flour lightly. Heat the remaining oil in a pan and fry the squid, turning until coloured on all sides.

5 Arrange the squid in the tomato sauce. Add the wine and bay leaf. Cover the pan tightly and simmer for 30 minutes. Serve sliced into rings, surrounded by the sauce and garnished with parsley.

Nutritional information per portion: Energy 441kcal/1844kJ; Protein 28.8g; Carbohydrate 27g, of which sugars 9.4g; Fat 20.1g, of which saturates 3.2g; Cholesterol 346mg; Calcium 84mg; Fibre 2.1g; Sodium 364mg.

Zarzuela

The name of this dish translates as "light musical comedy", reflecting the colour and variety of the stew, which is full of all sorts of fish and shellfish. It is distinguished from other fish stews by containing tomato as well as saffron. It's a splendid feast and not difficult to make.

SERVES 6

250g/9oz monkfish on the bone
1 gurnard, snapper or other whole white
    fish, about 350g/12oz, cleaned
1 sole, plaice or flounder or other whole
    flat fish, about 500g/1¼lb, cleaned
60ml/4 tbsp olive oil
8 small squid, with tentacles
plain (all-purpose) flour,
    for dusting
30ml/2 tbsp anis spirit, such as Ricard
    or Pernod
250ml/8fl oz/1 cup white wine
450g/1lb mussels, cleaned

4 large raw scampi (extra large shrimp),
    with heads
12 raw king prawns (jumbo shrimp),
    with heads
115g/4oz raw shelled prawns (shrimp)
salt and ground black pepper
45ml/3 tbsp chopped fresh parsley,
    to garnish

FOR THE STOCK
1 onion, chopped
1 celery stick, chopped
1 bay leaf

FOR THE FISH BROTH
30ml/2 tbsp oil
1 large onion, finely chopped
2 garlic cloves, finely chopped
500g/1¼lb ripe tomatoes, peeled,
    seeded and chopped
2 bay leaves
1 dried chilli, seeded and chopped
5ml/1 tsp paprika
pinch of saffron threads (0.2g)
salt and ground black pepper

1 Prepare the fish. Remove the flesh from the bones and cut into portions. You should have about 500g/1¼lb white fish, both firm and soft. Salt the fish and reserve on a plate in the refrigerator. (Reserve the bones and heads for making the stock.)

2 Make the stock. Put the onion, celery, bay leaf and the fish bones and heads in a pan, pour in 600ml/1 pint/2½ cups water, and bring to the boil, then simmer for about 30 minutes.

3 Make the broth in a large, heavy pan. Heat the oil and fry the onion and garlic gently until soft. Add the chopped tomatoes, bay leaves, dried chilli, paprika and crumbled saffron and cook gently to make a sauce.

4 To cook the fish and shellfish, heat the oil in a large frying pan. Put in the squid tentacles, face down, and cook for 45 seconds, to make "flowers". Reserve on a plate.

5 Flour and fry the monkfish and white fish for 3 minutes on each side, then the flat fish for 2 minutes on each side. Cut the squid bodies into rings and fry. Pour the anis spirit into a ladle, flame it and pour over the fish remaining in the pan. Remove the fish and reserve.

6 Strain the fish stock into the tomato sauce and add the wine. Bring to a simmer. Add the mussels in two batches. Cover for a couple of minutes, then remove to a plate, discard any closed mussels, and remove the upper shells.

7 Add the scampi and cook for about 8 minutes, then lift out using a slotted spoon. Cut with scissors along the underside from the head to the tail. Add the raw king prawns for 3–4 minutes, then lift out and reserve.

8 About 20 minutes before serving, assemble the casserole. Add the seafood to the hot broth in the following order, bringing the liquid back to simmering each time: firm white fish, soft white fish (with squid rings and pan juices), large shellfish in the shell, cooked shellfish in the shell, then any small shelled prawns. If the liquid level falls below the seafood, make it up with more wine. Check the seasonings.

9 Rearrange the soup with the best-looking shellfish and squid flowers on top. Scatter over the mussels, cover and leave to steam for 2 minutes. Garnish with parsley and serve.

Nutritional information per portion: Energy 326kcal/1367kJ; Protein 34.8g; Carbohydrate 5.4g, of which sugars 3.4g; Fat 14.4g, of which saturates 2.3g; Cholesterol 248mg; Calcium 79mg; Fibre 1g; Sodium 264mg.

Poultry, meat and game

From chicken in saffron rice to kidneys in sherry and the ever-popular meatballs in tomato sauce, there are dishes here for every occasion. Pork is a favourite meat, and lamb, veal, beef and rabbit are used widely. Poultry and game birds are immensely popular in Spain and may be stuffed with fruit, marinated in wine, cooked with seasonal vegetables or served in delicious sauces.

Orange chicken salad

With their tangy flavour, orange segments are the perfect partner for tender chicken in this tasty rice salad. To appreciate all the flavours fully, serve the salad at room temperature.

SERVES 4

3 large seedless oranges
175g/6oz/scant 1 cup long grain rice
175ml/6fl oz/³/₄ cup vinaigrette
10ml/2 tsp strong Dijon mustard
2.5ml/¹/₂ tsp caster (superfine) sugar
450g/1lb cooked chicken, diced
45ml/3 tbsp chopped fresh chives
75g/3oz/³/₄ cup almonds or cashew nuts, toasted
salt and ground black pepper
mixed salad leaves, to serve

1 Pare one of the oranges thinly, removing only the rind, not the pith. Put the pieces of orange rind in a pan and add the rice. Pour in 475ml/16fl oz/2 cups water, add a pinch of salt and bring to the boil. Cover and cook over a very low heat for 15 minutes, or until the rice is tender and the water has been absorbed.

2 Meanwhile, peel the oranges, removing all the pith. Separate them into segments over a plate. Add the orange juice from the plate to the

vinaigrette with the mustard and sugar, whisking to combine. Check the seasoning.

3 Discard the pieces of orange rind. from the cooked rice. Spoon the rice into a bowl, let it cool slightly, then add half the dressing. Toss well, then set aside to cool completely.

4 Add the chicken, chives, nuts and orange segments to the rice. Pour over the remaining dressing and toss. Serve on a bed of salad leaves.

Nutritional information per portion: Energy 642kcal/2678kJ; Protein 35.6g; Carbohydrate 49.5g, of which sugars 14g; Fat 33.7g, of which saturates 4.7g; Cholesterol 79mg; Calcium 118mg; Fibre 3.5g; Sodium 278mg.

Chicken with lemon and garlic

Pollo con limón y ajillo *is one of the simplest and most delicious ways to serve chicken. It makes a good tapas dish, served with cocktail sticks, or a supper for two, with fried potatoes.*

SERVES 2–4

2 skinless chicken breast fillets
30ml/2 tbsp olive oil
1 shallot, finely chopped
4 garlic cloves, finely chopped
5ml/1 tsp paprika
juice of 1 lemon
30ml/2 tbsp chopped fresh parsley
salt and ground black pepper
fresh flat leaf parsley, to garnish
lemon wedges, to serve

1 Remove the little fillet from the back of each breast. If the breast still looks fatter than a finger, bat it with a rolling pin to make it thinner. Slice all the chicken meat into strips.

2 Heat the oil in a large frying pan. Stir-fry the chicken strips with the shallot, garlic and paprika over a high heat for about 3 minutes until cooked through.

3 Add the lemon juice and parsley and season with salt and pepper to taste. Serve hot with lemon wedges, garnished with flat leaf parsley.

Nutritional information per portion: Energy 138kcal/579kJ; Protein 18.5g; Carbohydrate 1.5g, of which sugars 1.1g; Fat 6.5g, of which saturates 1g; Cholesterol 53mg; Calcium 30mg; Fibre 0.8g; Sodium 49mg.

Crumbed chicken with green mayonnaise

Pechugas de pollo rebozadas are sold ready-prepared in every butcher's in the South. Identical to schnitzel, these crispy, golden chicken breast portions show the Jewish influence on cooking in the region. Lemon wedges are a popular accompaniment.

SERVES 4

4 chicken breast fillets, each weighing
   about 200g/7oz
juice of 1 lemon
5ml/1 tsp paprika
plain (all-purpose) flour, for dusting
1–2 eggs
dried breadcrumbs, for coating
about 60ml/4 tbsp olive oil
salt and ground black pepper
lemon wedges, to serve (optional)

FOR THE MAYONNAISE
120ml/4fl oz/¹⁄₂ cup mayonnaise
30ml/2 tbsp pickled capers, drained
   and chopped
30ml/2 tbsp chopped fresh parsley

1 Start a couple of hours ahead, if you can. Skin the chicken fillets. Lay them outside down and, with a sharp knife, cut horizontally, almost through, from the rounded side. Open them up like a book. Press gently, to make a roundish shape, the size of a side plate. Sprinkle with lemon juice and paprika.

2 Set out three plates. Sprinkle flour over one, seasoning it well. Beat the egg with a little salt and pour into the second. Sprinkle the third with dried breadcrumbs. Dip the fillets first into the flour on both sides, then into the egg, then into the breadcrumbs. Chill the crumbed chicken, if you have time.

3 Put the mayonnaise ingredients in a bowl and mix well to combine.

4 Heat the oil in a heavy frying pan over a high heat. Fry the fillets, two at a time, turning after 3 minutes, until golden on both sides. Add more oil for the second batch if needed. Serve at once, with the mayonnaise and lemon wedges, if using.

Nutritional information per portion: Energy 594kcal/2476kJ; Protein 52g; Carbohydrate 12.5g, of which sugars 1.1g; Fat 37.7g, of which saturates 6g; Cholesterol 210mg; Calcium 64mg; Fibre 1g; Sodium 372mg.

Pollo a la Española

This colourful chicken dish is made throughout Spain in an infinite number of variations. Cubed Serrano ham can replace the bacon, but the fat the latter gives off is a constant theme in the Spanish kitchen, so helps to add to its character.

SERVES 4

5ml/1 tsp paprika
4 free-range or corn-fed chicken portions
45ml/3 tbsp olive oil
150g/5oz smoked bacon lardons,
   or diced pancetta
1 large onion, chopped
2 garlic cloves, finely chopped
1 green (bell) pepper
1 red (bell) pepper
450g/1lb tomatoes or 400g/14oz
   canned tomatoes
30ml/2 tbsp chopped fresh parsley
salt and ground black pepper
boiled rice, to serve (optional)

1 Rub paprika and salt into the chicken portions. Heat 30ml/2 tbsp oil in a large frying pan. Put in the chicken portions, skin side down, and fry gently.

2 Heat 15ml/1 tbsp oil in a large, heavy pan and then add the diced bacon or pancetta. When the bacon or pancetta starts to give off fat, add the chopped onion and garlic, frying very gently until soft.

3 Remove and discard the stalks and seeds from the peppers and chop the flesh. Spoon off a little fat from the chicken pan, then add the peppers, fitting them between the chicken portions, and cook over a gentle heat.

4 When the onions are soft, stir in the tomatoes and season. Arrange the chicken pieces in the sauce, and stir in the cooked peppers.

5 Cover the pan tightly and simmer over a low heat for 15 minutes. Check the seasoning, stir in the parsley and serve with rice, if you like.

Nutritional information per portion: Energy 365kcal/1529kJ; Protein 44.1g; Carbohydrate 9.6g, of which sugars 8.6g; Fat 16.9g, of which saturates 4.2g; Cholesterol 125mg; Calcium 36mg; Fibre 2.6g; Sodium 682mg.

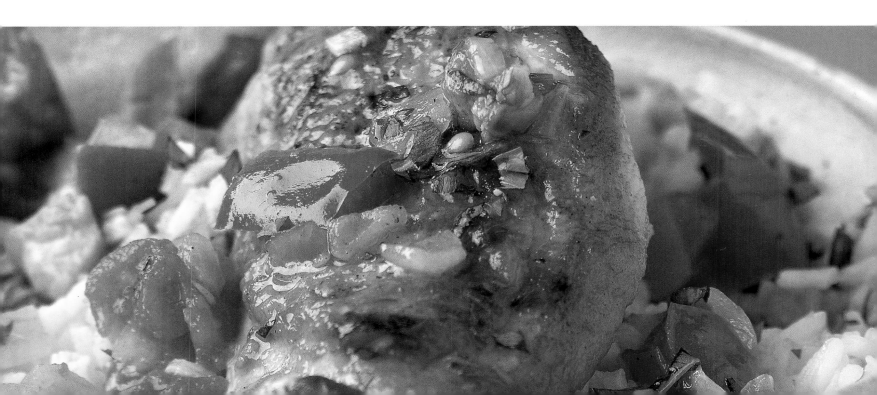

Arroz con pollo

Many Spanish families eat rice once a week, referring to it as arroz unless it is paella. This dish, rice with chicken, is cooked in one pot, with more liquid than a paella. Seasonal vegetables are included and peas and corn can be used.

SERVES 4

60ml/4 tbsp olive oil

6 chicken thighs, halved along the bone

5ml/1 tsp paprika

1 large Spanish onion, roughly chopped

2 garlic cloves, finely chopped

1 chorizo sausage, sliced

115g/4oz Serrano or cooked ham or
 gammon, diced

1 red (bell) pepper, seeded and
 roughly chopped

1 yellow (bell) pepper, seeded and
 roughly chopped

225g/8oz/1 generous cup paella rice,
 washed and drained

2 large tomatoes, chopped or 200g/7oz
 can chopped tomatoes

120ml/4fl oz/1/2 cup amontillado
 sherry

750ml/1¼ pints/3 cups chicken stock

5ml/1 tsp dried oregano or thyme

1 bay leaf

salt and ground black pepper

15 green olives and chopped fresh flat
 leaf parsley, to garnish

1 Heat the oil in a large, heavy pan or flameproof casserole dish. Season the chicken pieces with salt and paprika. Fry until nicely brown all over, then reserve on a plate.

2 Add the onion and garlic to the pan and fry gently until beginning to soften. Add the chorizo and ham or gammon and stir-fry. Add the chopped peppers. Cook until they begin to soften.

3 Sprinkle in the drained rice and cook, stirring, for 1–2 minutes. Add the tomatoes, sherry, chicken stock and dried herbs and season well. Arrange the chicken pieces deep in the mixture, and tuck in the bay leaf.

4 Cover and cook over a very low heat for 30–40 minutes, until the chicken and rice are done. Stir, then garnish and serve.

Nutritional information per portion: Energy 654kcal/2736kJ; Protein 49.7g; Carbohydrate 59.3g, of which sugars 11.2g; Fat 20.6g, of which saturates 5g; Cholesterol 132mg; Calcium 52mg; Fibre 2.8g; Sodium 651mg.

Pollo con langostinos

Chicken with prawns is another gorgeous Catalan dish. The sauce is thickened with a picada *or paste of ground toasted almonds, which is more convenient than making a roux. This special* picada *traditionally includes butter biscuit rather than the bread that normally goes into* picada.

SERVES 4

1.3kg/3lb free-range chicken
75–90ml/5–6 tbsp olive oil
1 large onion, chopped
2 garlic cloves, finely chopped
400g/14oz tomatoes, peeled and seeded
  then chopped or 400g/14oz can
  tomatoes, drained
1 bay leaf
150ml/1/4 pint/2/3 cup dry white wine
450g/1lb large raw prawns (shrimp), or
  16 large shelled prawn tails
15g/1/2oz/1 tbsp butter
30ml/2 tbsp anis spirit, such as Ricard
  or Pernod

75ml/21/2fl oz/1/3 cup double
  (heavy) cream
1.5ml/1/4 tsp cayenne pepper
salt, paprika and ground black pepper
fresh flat leaf parsley, to garnish
boiled rice or raw spinach salad, to serve

FOR THE *PICADA*
25g/1oz/1/4 cup blanched almonds
15g/1/2oz/1 tbsp butter
1 garlic clove, finely chopped
3 Marie, Rich Tea or plain all-butter
  biscuits (cookies), broken
90ml/6 tbsp chopped fresh parsley

1 Cut the chicken into eight serving portions, then separate the small fillet from the back of each breast portion. Rub salt and paprika into the chicken.

2 Heat 30ml/2 tbsp oil in a large, heavy pan and fry the onion and garlic until soft. Put in the chicken pieces, skinside down, and fry over a medium heat, turning until they are golden on all sides.

3 To make the *picada*, dry-fry the almonds in a frying pan, shaking it regularly, until they are coloured. Transfer them to a blender and process until smooth.

4 Add the butter to the pan and gently fry the garlic, then add it to the blender, with the broken biscuits. Reduce the biscuits to crumbs then add the chopped parsley and blend to a purée, adding a little of the wine intended for the casserole.

5 Add the tomatoes to the chicken, tuck in the bay leaf and cook down to a sauce, stirring occasionally. Pour in the remaining wine, season to taste with salt and ground black pepper, and leave to simmer gently.

6 Check the shelled prawn tails, if using: if they have a black thread along the back, nick it out with a knife. Heat 15ml/1 tbsp oil and the butter in the frying pan and add the prawns. Cook over a medium heat for 2 minutes on each side.

7 Pour the anis spirit into a ladle and set light to it. Off the heat, pour this over the prawns and let it burn off. Stir in the juices from the chicken, then transfer the contents back to the chicken pan.

8 Remove the bay leaf from the pan and stir in the *picada*, then the cream. Add cayenne to taste and check the seasonings, adding a little more if necessary. Heat through gently and serve garnished with parsley.

Nutritional information per portion: Energy 881kcal/3655kJ; Protein 52.5g; Carbohydrate 9.8g, of which sugars 4.1g; Fat 65.8g, of which saturates 22g; Cholesterol 368mg; Calcium 110mg; Fibre 1.7g; Sodium 934mg.

Chicken casserole with spiced figs

The Catalans have a reputation for serving fruit with poultry and meat. Here pollo con higos *is cooked with a beautifully spiced sauce, which goes perfectly with a Catalan Cabernet Sauvignon.*

SERVES 4

50g/2oz bacon lardons or pancetta, diced
15ml/1 tbsp olive oil
1.3–1.6kg/3–3¹/₂lb free-range or corn-
   fed chicken, jointed into eight pieces
120ml/4fl oz/¹/₂ cup white wine
finely pared rind of ¹/₂ lemon
50ml/2fl oz/¹/₄ cup chicken stock
salt and ground black pepper
green salad, to serve

FOR THE FIGS
150g/5oz/³/₄ cup sugar
120ml/4fl oz/¹/₂ cup white wine vinegar
1 lemon slice
1 cinnamon stick
120ml/4fl oz/¹/₂ cup water
450g/1lb fresh figs

1 Prepare the figs. Gently simmer the sugar, vinegar, lemon and cinnamon with the water for 5 minutes. Add the figs and cook for 10 minutes. Remove from the heat and leave to stand for 3 hours.

2 Fry the bacon or pancetta in a frying pan until golden. Transfer to an ovenproof dish. Add the oil to the pan. Season the chicken, brown on both sides, then transfer to the ovenproof dish.

3 Preheat the oven to 180°C/350°F/Gas 4. Drain the figs. Add the wine and lemon rind to the pan and boil until the wine has reduced and is syrupy. Pour over the chicken.

4 Cook the chicken in the oven, uncovered, for about 20 minutes, then add the figs and chicken stock. Cover and return to the oven for a further 10 minutes. Serve with a green salad.

Nutritional information per portion: Energy 811kcal/3396kJ; Protein 44g; Carbohydrate 69.8g, of which sugars 69.8g; Fat 39.2g, of which saturates 10.9g; Cholesterol 215mg; Calcium 183mg; Fibre 4.3g; Sodium 394mg.

Chicken chilindrón

This famous chicken dish from Navarra has a spicy red pepper sauce. In the past, the dried choricero *pepper was used alone, but fresh red peppers spiced with chilli are used nowadays.*

SERVES 4

675g/1¹/₂lb red (bell) peppers
4 free-range chicken portions
10ml/2 tsp paprika
30ml/2 tbsp olive oil
1 large onion, chopped
2 garlic cloves, finely chopped
200g/7oz Serrano or other ham, in one
  piece, or a gammon chop, diced
200g/7oz can chopped tomatoes
1 dried *guindilla* **or other hot dried chilli,**
  chopped, or 2.5ml/¹/₂ tsp chilli
  powder, to taste
salt and ground black pepper
chopped fresh parsley, to garnish
small new potatoes, to serve

1 Preheat the grill (broiler) to high. Put the peppers on a baking sheet and grill (broil) for 8–12 minutes, until the skins have blackened, turning every so often. Place in a bowl, cover with clear film (plastic wrap) and leave to cool.

2 Rub salt and paprika into the chicken portions. Heat the oil in a large frying pan and add the chicken portions, skinside down. Fry over a medium-low heat, turning until golden on all sides.

3 Spoon 45ml/3 tbsp fat from the frying pan into a large, heavy pan. Fry the onion and garlic until soft. Add the ham or gammon, stirring occasionally, for a few minutes. Add the chopped tomatoes to the pan, with the chilli or chilli powder. Cook for 4–5 minutes, letting the sauce reduce.

4 Peel the skins off the peppers and discard these and the stalks. Put the peppers into a blender and strain in the juices, discarding the seeds. Process, then add to the pan and stir in. Heat through, then add the chicken pieces. Cook, covered, for 15 minutes and check the seasonings. Garnish with a little parsley and serve with small new potatoes.

Nutritional information per portion: Energy 332kcal/1396kJ; Protein 47.6g; Carbohydrate 13.8g, of which sugars 12.4g; Fat 10g, of which saturates 2.1g; Cholesterol 134mg; Calcium 33mg; Fibre 3.2g; Sodium 702mg.

Roast turkey with black fruit stuffing

Columbus introduced turkeys from America to Spain, and at first they were cooked like peacocks – stuffed, then roasted inside a pig's caul.

SERVES 8

3kg/6^1/$_2$lb bronze or black turkey,
   weighed without the giblets
60ml/4 tbsp oil
200g/7oz rashers (strips) streaky
   (fatty) bacon

FOR THE STUFFING
30ml/2 tbsp olive oil
1 onion, chopped
2 garlic cloves, finely chopped
115g/4oz fatty bacon lardons
150g/5oz *morcilla* or black pudding
   (blood sausage), diced
1 turkey liver, diced
50g/2oz/^{1}/$_2$ cup Muscatel raisins, soaked
   in 45ml/3 tbsp anis spirit, such as
   Ricard, and chopped
115g/4oz ready-to-eat pitted prunes,
   chopped

50g/2oz/^{1}/$_2$ cup almonds, chopped
1.5ml/^{1}/$_4$ tsp dried thyme
finely grated rind of 1 lemon
freshly grated nutmeg
60ml/4 tbsp chopped fresh parsley
1 large (US extra large) egg, beaten
60ml/4 tbsp cooked rice or stale
   breadcrumbs
salt and ground black pepper

FOR THE SAUCE
45ml/3 tbsp plain (all-purpose) flour
350ml/12fl oz/1^1/$_2$ cups turkey giblet
   stock, warmed
350ml/12fl oz/1^1/$_2$ cups red grape juice
30ml/2 tbsp anis spirit, such as Ricard
salt and ground black pepper

1 Make the stuffing. Heat the oil in a pan and fry the onion, garlic and bacon. Remove to a large bowl. Fry the *morcilla* or black pudding for 3–4 minutes and the liver for 2–3 minutes.

2 Add the soaked raisins, prunes, almonds, thyme, lemon rind, nutmeg, seasoning and parsley. Stir in the egg and rice or breadcrumbs.

3 About 3 hours before carving, preheat the oven, with a low shelf, to 200°C/400°F/Gas 6. Remove the turkey's wishbone, running fingernails up the two sides of the neck to find it. Just nick it out. Season the turkey inside, stuff and retruss it. Season outside. Keep at room temperature.

4 Heat a roasting pan in the oven with 60ml/4 tbsp oil. Put in the turkey and baste the outside. Lay the bacon over the breast and legs. Reduce the oven temperature to 180°C/350°F/Gas 4 and roast for 2^1/$_4$–2^1/$_2$ hours, basting once.

5 To test, insert a skewer into the thickest part of the inside leg. The juices should run clear. Remove the trussing thread and transfer the turkey to a heated serving plate. Keep warm.

6 Make the sauce. Skim as much fat as possible from the roasting pan. Sprinkle in the flour and cook gently for a few minutes, stirring. Stir in the warm turkey stock and bring to simmering point. Add the grape juice and anis, and bring back to simmering. Taste for seasoning. Pour into a jug (pitcher). Carve the turkey and serve with the sauce.

Nutritional information per portion: Energy 662kcal/2772kJ; Protein 66.3g; Carbohydrate 27.9g, of which sugars 15.5g; Fat 31.5g, of which saturates 8.1g; Cholesterol 274mg; Calcium 104mg; Fibre 2.2g; Sodium 658mg.

Spiced duck with pears

This Catalan speciality is a fabulous combination of poultry and fruit. This dish features the picada, a great Catalan invention made of pounded nuts, which both flavours and thickens the final sauce. Serve with a bottle of Gran Sangre de Toro.

SERVES 6

6 duck portions, preferably Barbary,
    either breast portions or leg pieces
1 large onion, thinly sliced
1 cinnamon stick, halved
4 thyme sprigs
475ml/16fl oz/2 cups duck or
    chicken stock
3 firm, ripe pears
30ml/2 tbsp olive oil
25g/1oz/1/4 cup raisins
salt and ground black pepper
young thyme sprigs or fresh parsley,
    to garnish

mashed potatoes and green vegetables,
    to serve (optional)

FOR THE *PICADA*
30ml/2 tbsp olive oil
1/2 slice stale bread, without crusts
2 garlic cloves, sliced
15g/1/2oz/12 almonds, toasted
15g/1/2oz/12 hazelnuts, toasted
15ml/1 tbsp chopped fresh parsley
salt and ground black pepper

1 Preheat the oven to 180°C/350°F/Gas 4. Season the duck portions, pricking the skins with a fork. Fry them, skinside down, for about 5 minutes, until they give off fat. Turn them over and fry on the other side more briefly.

2 Transfer the duck to an ovenproof dish and drain off all but 15ml/1 tbsp of the fat left in the pan.

3 Add the onion to the pan and fry for 5 minutes. Add the cinnamon, thyme and stock and bring to the boil. Pour over the duck, reserving a little of the stock, and bake for 1¼ hours.

4 Meanwhile, make the *picada*. Heat the olive oil in a frying pan and fry the bread over a high heat. Drain on kitchen paper and reserve. Briefly fry the garlic and reserve with the bread.

5 Put all the nuts in a mortar and pound, or reduce to a paste in a food processor or blender. Add the bread, torn into pieces, and the garlic, and reduce to a thick, smooth paste with a little pan stock. Add the parsley and seasoning.

6 Peel, core and halve the pears. Fry quickly in the oil in the frying pan until beginning to colour on the cut sides.

7 Add the *picada* to the ovenproof dish with the raisins and pears. Bake for a further 15 minutes until the pears are tender. Season to taste and garnish with thyme or parsley. Serve with mashed potatoes and vegetables, if you wish.

Nutritional information per portion: Energy 296kcal/1235kJ; Protein 21.5g; Carbohydrate 14.7g, of which sugars 11.3g; Fat 18.8g, of which saturates 2.8g; Cholesterol 110mg; Calcium 40mg; Fibre 2.3g; Sodium 147mg.

Guinea fowl with saffron and nut sauce

The Arabs introduced saffron to Spain and this is a Moorish sauce. **Pepita** *is the Spanish word for a seed or nut, hence the name* **pintada en pepitoria**. *Serve with a Rioja Reserva.*

SERVES 4

25g/1oz/¼ cup blanched almonds
pinch of saffron threads (0.1g)
120ml/4 fl oz/½ cup chicken stock
1.2–1.3kg/2½–3lb guinea fowl
60ml/4fl oz/¼ cup olive oil
1 thick slice of bread, without crusts
2 garlic cloves, finely chopped
120ml/4fl oz/½ cup fino sherry
1 bay leaf, crumbled
4 thyme sprigs
15ml/1 tbsp finely chopped fresh parsley
pinch of freshly grated nutmeg
pinch of ground cloves
juice of ½ lemon
5ml/1 tsp paprika
salt and ground black pepper

1 Preheat the oven to 150°C/300°F/Gas 2. Spread the almonds on a baking sheet and toast in the oven for about 20 minutes. Crumble the saffron into a small bowl, pour over 30ml/2 tbsp hot chicken stock and leave to soak.

2 Cut the bird into eight serving pieces, discarding the wing tips, backbone, breastbones and leg tips. This will give you two legs (split them at the joint), two wings with one-third of the breast attached, and two short breast pieces.

3 Heat the olive oil in a large, heavy pan and fry the bread slice on both sides. Fry the garlic quickly, then remove both to a blender.

4 Season the poultry well and fry them, turning until golden on all sides. Add the remaining stock and the sherry to the pan, stirring to deglaze the pan. Add the bay leaf and thyme and cover. Cook gently for 10 minutes.

5 Grind together the bread, garlic and almonds. Add the parsley, saffron liquid, nutmeg and cloves, and purée. Stir into the poultry juices, add the lemon juice and paprika, season and serve.

Nutritional information per portion: Energy 589kcal/2442kJ; Protein 38.6g; Carbohydrate 4.2g, of which sugars 0.9g; Fat 42.8g, of which saturates 10.5g; Cholesterol 192mg; Calcium 40mg; Fibre 0.6g; Sodium 189mg.

Perdices con uvas

Partridges are Spain's commonest game birds. They have a natural affinity with grapes which are used for the garnish and sauce in this dish. Game hens or any plump small bird can also be used.

SERVES 4

4 partridges, cleaned
500g/1¼lb red grapes, split and seeded,
   plus extra to garnish
45–60ml/3–4 tbsp olive oil
4 rashers (slices) smoked streaky (fatty)
   bacon, halved across
1 onion, chopped
2 garlic cloves, finely chopped
1 bay leaf
120ml/4fl oz/½ cup dry white wine
250ml/8fl oz/1 cup game or chicken
   stock
freshly grated nutmeg
salt and ground black pepper
30ml/2 tbsp chopped fresh parsley,
   to garnish

1 Season the birds inside and out, then stuff with 250g/9oz grapes. Put 45ml/3 tbsp oil in a large, heavy pan into which the birds will fit snugly.

2 Fry the bacon until crisp, then reserve on a plate. Put the birds into the pan breast sides down and fry until coloured. Turn them with two spoons, frying and turning until brown all over. Remove.

3 Fry the onion and garlic, adding a little more oil if needed, until softened. Return the birds to the casserole and put two pieces of bacon on top of each. Push 125g/5oz grapes in round them, and add the bay leaf. Pour in the white wine and stock. Add plenty of black pepper. Simmer, covered, for 30 minutes.

4 Remove the birds and bacon to a plate. Spoon the pan contents into a food processor. Discard the bay leaf, and purée. Add the nutmeg and season.

5 Return the birds to the pan, pour the sauce around them, and add 125g/5oz grapes. Heat through. Serve, garnished with extra grapes, crumbled bacon and a little parsley.

Nutritional information per portion: Energy 832kcal/3494kJ; Protein 125.6g; Carbohydrate 15.6g, of which sugars 15.6g; Fat 27.9g, of which saturates 7.6g; Cholesterol 13mg; Calcium 171mg; Fibre 0.7g; Sodium 718mg.

Braised quail with winter vegetables

Quail are both plentiful and very popular in Spain, especially during the hunting season. Here, in cordonices estofadas, *they are cooked and served in a red wine sauce.*

SERVES 4

4 quail, cleaned
60ml/4 tbsp olive oil
175g/6oz small carrots, cut into chunks
175g/6oz baby turnips, cut into chunks
4 shallots, halved
450ml/¾ pint/scant 2 cups red wine
30ml/2 tbsp Spanish brandy
salt and ground black pepper
fresh flat leaf parsley, to garnish

FOR THE CROÛTES
4 slices stale bread, crusts removed
60ml/4 tbsp olive oil

1 Preheat the oven to 220°C/ 425°F/Gas 7. Season the quail with salt and ground black pepper.

2 Heat half the oil in a flameproof casserole and add the quail. Fry until browned all over. Remove from the casserole and set aside.

3 Add more oil to the casserole with all the vegetables and shallots. Cook until just colouring. Return the quail to the casserole, breast sides down, and add the wine. Cover and transfer to the oven. Cook for 30 minutes, or until the quail are tender.

4 Using a 10cm/4in plain cutter stamp out rounds from the bread. Heat the oil in a frying pan and cook the bread over a high heat until golden on both sides. Drain on kitchen paper and keep warm.

5 Place the croûtes on plates and set a quail on top of each. Arrange the vegetables around the quail.

6 Boil the cooking juices hard until reduced to a syrupy consistency. Add the brandy and warm through, then season. Drizzle over the quail and garnish with parsley, then serve.

Nutritional information per portion: Energy 591kcal/2456kJ; Protein 24.4g; Carbohydrate 14.3g, of which sugars 6.7g; Fat 38.8g, of which saturates 7.6g; Cholesterol 116mg; Calcium 68mg; Fibre 2.5g; Sodium 184mg.

Marinated pigeon in red wine

Migrating pigeons fly over the mountains of Spain twice a year, and shooting them is a big sport. Here they are marinated in spiced vinegar and red wine, then cooked in the marinade.

SERVES 4

4 pigeons (squabs), each about
    225g/8oz, cleaned
30ml/2 tbsp olive oil
1 onion, roughly chopped
225g/8oz/3 cups brown cap (cremini)
    mushrooms, sliced
plain (all-purpose) flour, for dusting
300ml/½ pint/1¼ cups beef or
    game stock
30ml/2 tbsp chopped fresh parsley
salt and ground black pepper
fresh flat leaf parsley, to garnish

FOR THE MARINADE
15ml/1 tbsp olive oil
1 onion, chopped
1 carrot, chopped
1 celery stick, chopped
3 garlic cloves, sliced
6 allspice berries, bruised
2 bay leaves
8 black peppercorns, bruised
120ml/4fl oz/1/2 cup red wine vinegar
150ml/1/4 pint/2/3 cup red wine

1 Starting a day ahead, combine all the ingredients for the marinade in a large dish. Add the pigeons and turn them in the marinade. Cover and chill for 12 hours. Turn occasionally.

2 Preheat the oven to 150°C/300°F/Gas 2. Heat the oil in a large, flameproof casserole and cook the onion and mushrooms for about 5 minutes, until the onion has softened.

3 Meanwhile, remove the pigeons to a plate with a slotted spoon and strain the marinade into a bowl, then set both aside separately.

4 Sprinkle the flour on the pigeons and add them to the casserole, breast sides down. Pour in the marinade and stock, and add the chopped parsley and seasoning. Cover and cook in the oven for 1½ hours or until tender.

5 Check the seasoning, then serve the pigeons on warmed plates with the sauce. Garnish with the fresh parsley leaves.

Nutritional information per portion: Energy 286kcal/1189kJ; Protein 25.6g; Carbohydrate 1.5g, of which sugars 1g; Fat 17.4g, of which saturates 0.9g; Cholesterol 0mg; Calcium 23mg; Fibre 0.8g; Sodium 98mg.

Liver and bacon casserole

In Spain, liver means pig's liver, and is cooked here in a well-seasoned sauce. The pig's liver is the first thing to be eaten from the new pig, and so is associated with one of the big feasts of the year, Matanza. You can substitute lamb's liver if you prefer.

SERVES 3–4

450g/1lb pig's or lamb's liver, trimmed
   and sliced
60ml/4 tbsp milk (for pig's liver)
30ml/2 tbsp olive oil
225g/8oz rindless smoked lean bacon rashers
   (strips), cut into pieces
2 onions, halved and sliced
175g/6oz/2¼ cups brown cap (cremini)
   mushrooms, halved

25g/1oz/2 tbsp butter
30ml/2 tbsp plain (all-purpose) flour
150ml/¼ pint/⅔ cup hot chicken stock
15ml/1 tbsp soy sauce
5ml/1 tsp paprika
salt and ground black pepper

1 If using pig's liver, soak it in the milk for about 1 hour for a milder flavour, then blot the pig's liver dry with kitchen paper.

2 Heat the oil in a frying pan and stir-fry the bacon until crisp. Add the onion and cook, stirring, until softened. Add the mushrooms and fry for 1 minute.

3 Using a slotted spoon, remove the bacon and vegetables from the pan and keep warm. Add the liver to the fat remaining in the pan and cook over a high heat for 3–4 minutes, turning once to seal the slices on both sides. Remove from the pan and keep warm.

4 Melt the butter in the pan, sprinkle the flour over and cook briefly. Stir in the stock, soy sauce and paprika and bring to a simmer. Return the liver and vegetables. Simmer gently for 3–4 minutes. Check the seasoning.

Nutritional information per portion: Energy 386kcal/1610kJ; Protein 35.3g; Carbohydrate 8g, of which sugars 1.4g; Fat 23.9g, of which saturates 8.7g; Cholesterol 336mg; Calcium 29mg; Fibre 0.9g; Sodium 1267mg.

Fabada

This bean and sausage hotpot from the wild mountains of Asturias on the northern coast of Spain, has achieved world fame. It used to contain dried broad beans, which gave it the name, but when modern fabes – white kidney beans – were adopted, it became a truly great dish.

SERVES 8

500–800g/1¼–1¾lb belly pork, in thick slices
1 smoked gammon (smoked or cured ham) knuckle, about 675g/1½lb, skin slashed
800g/1¾lb dried cannellini beans, soaked overnight
5ml/1 tsp black peppercorns, crushed
15ml/1 tbsp paprika

pinch of saffron threads (0.2g)
1 bay leaf
30ml/2 tbsp oil (optional)
4 garlic cloves, chopped
3 red chorizo sausages, thickly sliced
175g/6oz *morcilla* or black pudding (blood sausage), thickly sliced
ground black pepper (optional)

1 Put the pork belly and knuckle into a very large stockpot with water to cover. Bring to the boil, then drain the meat and return it to the stockpot.

2 Add the drained beans to the pot and pour over 2.3 litres/4 pints/10 cups water. Bring to the boil very slowly, then boil for 10 minutes. Reduce the heat and add the peppercorns, paprika, crumbled saffron and the bay leaf. Simmer very gently over a very low heat for 2 hours. Check occasionally that the beans are still covered with liquid, but stir carefully or the beans will break up.

3 Remove the pork belly and knuckle and set them aside to cool. Strip off the skin and fat, and take 30ml/2 tbsp chopped fat for frying (or use oil). Heat this in a frying pan and cook the garlic lightly, then spoon it into the beans. Fry the chorizo and *morcilla* or black pudding lightly in the pan. Gently stir into the bean pot.

4 Remove all the meat from the ham bone. Chop it with the pork and return to the stockpot. Simmer for a few minutes. Check the seasonings and serve.

COOK'S TIP
The quality of the bean is a feature of the dish so try to use luxury Spanish beans. **Fabes** *are like very large, white cannellini beans. If luxury Spanish beans are unavailable use* lingots *(the French cassoulet bean).*

Nutritional information per portion: Energy 741kcal/3106kJ; Protein 46.4g; Carbohydrate 59.6g, of which sugars 3.2g; Fat 36.9g, of which saturates 13.7g; Cholesterol 79mg; Calcium 106mg; Fibre 8.3g; Sodium 918mg.

Chorizo with cooked chestnuts

Native to Galicia, chestnuts are a popular addition to a variety of dishes. Chorizos y castanas makes a good side dish for roast turkey and a popular supper dish on its own. Add a little chilli for heat and spiciness.

SERVES 3–6

15ml/1 tbsp olive oil
4 red chorizo sausages, sliced
200g/7oz/1¼ cups peeled cooked chestnuts
15ml/1 tbsp paprika
salt and ground black pepper
crusty bread, to serve

1 Heat the oil in a wide frying pan and put in the chorizo slices in a single layer. Cook the chorizo for 3–4 minutes, turning frequently, until it starts to give off its oil.

2 Tip in the peeled chestnuts and toss until warm and covered with the chorizo oil. Add the paprika and season with the salt and ground black pepper. Serve hot with crusty bread.

Nutritional information per portion: Energy 180kcal/752kJ; Protein 4.2g; Carbohydrate 17g, of which sugars 2.9g; Fat 11.1g, of which saturates 3.8g; Cholesterol 13mg; Calcium 36mg; Fibre 1.5g; Sodium 275mg.

Albóndigas con salsa de tomate

These tasty meatballs in tomato sauce are usually served in little brown, individual casserole dishes, accompanied by crusty bread. They also make a good supper dish, with a green salad or pasta.

SERVES 4

225g/8oz minced (ground) beef
4 spring onions (scallions), thinly sliced
2 garlic cloves, finely chopped
30ml/2 tbsp grated fresh Parmesan cheese
10ml/2 tsp fresh thyme leaves
15ml/1 tbsp olive oil
3 tomatoes, chopped
30ml/2 tbsp red or dry white wine
10ml/2 tsp chopped fresh rosemary
pinch of sugar
salt and ground black pepper
fresh thyme, to garnish

1 Put the minced beef in a bowl. Add the spring onions, garlic, Parmesan and thyme and of salt and pepper. Stir to mix, then shape the mixture into 12 small firm balls.

2 Heat the olive oil in a large, heavy frying pan and cook the meatballs for about 5 minutes, turning frequently, until evenly browned all over. Add the chopped tomatoes, wine, rosemary and sugar to the pan, with salt and ground black pepper to taste.

3 Cover the pan and cook gently for about 15 minutes until the meatballs are cooked through. Check the seasoning and serve, garnished with the thyme.

Nutritional information per portion: Energy 206kcal/856kJ; Protein 14.4g; Carbohydrate 5.2g, of which sugars 5.1g; Fat 13.8g, of which saturates 5.5g; Cholesterol 38mg; Calcium 121mg; Fibre 1.5g; Sodium 133mg.

Black bean stew

Tolosa in the Basque country is famous for its black bean stew – potaje de alubias negras – made spicy with sausages and pickled pork. Here is a simplified version, with extra fresh vegetables.

SERVES 5–6

275g/10oz/1¹/₂ cups black beans, soaked
    overnight in cold water
675g/1¹/₂lb boneless belly pork
    rashers (strips)
60ml/4 tbsp olive oil
350g/12oz baby (pearl) onions
2 celery sticks, thickly sliced
150g/5oz chorizo, cut into chunks
10ml/2 tsp paprika
600ml/1 pint/2¹/₂ cups light chicken or
    vegetable stock
2 green (bell) peppers, seeded and cut
    into large pieces
salt and ground black pepper

1 Drain the beans into a pan and cover with fresh water. Bring to the boil and boil rapidly for 10 minutes. Drain the beans and put in an ovenproof dish.

2 Preheat the oven to 160°C/325°F/Gas 3. Cut away any rind from the pork, then cut it into large chunks.

3 Heat the oil in a large frying pan and fry the onions and celery for 3 minutes. Add the pork and fry for 10 minutes, or until the pork is browned.

4 Add the chorizo and fry for 2 minutes, then sprinkle in the paprika. Tip the mixture into the beans and mix well to combine thoroughly.

5 Add the stock to the pan and bring to the boil, then pour over the meat and beans. Cover and bake for 1 hour.

6 Stir the green peppers into the stew and return to the oven for a further 15 minutes. Season and serve hot.

Nutritional information per portion: Energy 760kcal/3159kJ; Protein 32.1g; Carbohydrate 37.3g, of which sugars 9.2g; Fat 54.7g, of which saturates 18.6g; Cholesterol 91mg; Calcium 85mg; Fibre 5.9g; Sodium 303mg.

Stuffed roast loin of pork

Pork is Spain's most popular meat, particularly the loin. For this dish, lomo de cerdo relleno, *you need the whole cut with the flap on the side to enclose the stuffing, which is flavoured with figs.*

SERVES 4

60ml/4 tbsp olive oil
1 onion, finely chopped
2 garlic cloves, chopped
75g/3oz/1½ cups stale breadcrumbs
4 ready-to-eat dried figs, chopped
8 pitted green olives, chopped
25g/1oz/¼ cup flaked (sliced) almonds
15ml/1 tbsp lemon juice
15ml/1 tbsp chopped fresh parsley
1 egg yolk
1kg/2¼lb boned loin of pork with the side flap attached
salt, paprika and ground black pepper

1 Preheat the oven to 200°C/400°F/Gas 6. Heat 45ml/3 tbsp of the oil in a pan, add the onion and garlic, and cook gently until softened. Remove the pan from the heat, and stir in the breadcrumbs, figs, olives, almonds, lemon juice, parsley and egg yolk. Season with salt, paprika and pepper.

2 Remove any string from the pork and unroll the belly flap, cutting away any excess fat or meat to enable you to do so. Spread half the stuffing over the flat piece and roll it up, starting from the thick side. Tie the joint at intervals with string to hold it together.

3 Pour the remaining oil into a small roasting pan and add the pork. Roast for 1¼ hours. Meanwhile, form the remaining stuffing mixture into balls and add to the pan, 15–20 minutes before the end of cooking time.

4 Remove the pork from the oven and leave it to rest for 10 minutes. Carve into thick slices and serve with the stuffing balls and any juices from the pan. This dish is also good served cold.

Nutritional information per portion: Energy 732kcal/3065kJ; Protein 80.3g; Carbohydrate 25.6g, of which sugars 11.3g; Fat 34.9g, of which saturates 8.5g; Cholesterol 245mg; Calcium 133mg; Fibre 2.7g; Sodium 592mg.

Pork empanada

This flat, two-crust Galician pie is famous because there is no occasion on which it is not served. It is festival food; it greets the boats of returning fishermen; and it is the men's lunchbox staple. Fillings vary enormously, and may include fish such as sardines, or scallops for special occasions.

SERVES 8

75ml/5 tbsp olive oil

2 onions, chopped

4 garlic cloves, finely chopped

1kg/2¼lb boned pork loin, diced

175g/6oz smoked gammon (smoked or
   cured ham) or raw ham, diced

3 red chorizo or other spicy sausages,
   about 300g/11oz

3 (bell) peppers mixed colours, seeded
   and chopped

175ml/6fl oz/¾ cup white wine

200g/7oz can tomatoes

pinch of saffron threads (0.1g)

5ml/1 tsp paprika

30ml/2 tbsp chopped fresh parsley

salt and ground black pepper

FOR THE CORNMEAL DOUGH

250g/9oz cornmeal

7g/2 tsp easy-blend (rapid-rise) dried yeast

5ml/1 tsp caster (superfine) sugar

250g/9oz plain (all-purpose) flour, plus extra
   for dusting

5ml/1 tsp salt

200ml/7fl oz/scant 1 cup warm water

30ml/2 tbsp oil

2 eggs, beaten, plus 1 for the glaze

1 Make the filling. Heat 60ml/4 tbsp oil in a frying pan and fry the onions, adding the garlic when the onions begin to colour. Transfer to a flameproof casserole. Add the pork and gammon or ham to the pan, and fry until coloured, stirring. Transfer to the casserole.

2 Add 15ml/1 tbsp oil, the sausage and the peppers to the pan and fry. Transfer to the casserole. Deglaze the pan with the wine, allowing it to bubble and reduce. Pour into the casserole.

3 Add the tomatoes, saffron, paprika and parsley and season. Cook gently for 20–30 minutes. Leave to cool.

4 Meanwhile make the dough. Put the cornmeal into a food processor. Add the dried yeast with the sugar. Gradually add the flour, salt, water, oil and two eggs and beat, to make a smooth soft dough.

5 Turn the dough into a clean bowl, cover with a dishtowel and leave in a warm place for 40–50 minutes, to rise.

6 Preheat the oven to 200°C/400°F/Gas 6. Grease a shallow roasting pan or dish 30 x 20cm/12 x 8in. Halve the dough. Roll out one half on a floured surface, a little larger than the pan. Lift this in place, leaving the border hanging over the edge.

7 Spoon in the filling. Roll out the lid and lay it in place. Fold the outside edge over the lid, trimming as necessary, and press gently all round with a fork to seal the pie. Prick the surface and brush with beaten egg.

8 Bake the pie for 30–35 minutes until golden, covering the ends if they brown too much. Cut the pie into squares.

Nutritional information per portion: Energy 704kcal/2944kJ; Protein 35.5g; Carbohydrate 58.6g, of which sugars 6.5g; Fat 35.6g, of which saturates 12.2g; Cholesterol 129mg; Calcium 97mg; Fibre 3.2g; Sodium 592mg.

Cocido

The Spanish national dish, cocido, *is also Madrid's most famous stew. The name simply means "boiled dinner" and it used to be made more than once a week. The broth makes a soup course and then the rest is displayed on two splendid platters.*

SERVES 8

500–800g/1¼–1¾lb cured brisket or
   silverside (pot roast)
250g/9oz smoked streaky (fatty) bacon,
   in one piece, or 250g/9oz belly pork
1 knuckle gammon (smoked or cured ham)
   bone, with some meat still attached
500–750g/1¼–1¾lb beef marrow bone,
   sawn through
1 pig's trotter (foot), sawn through
1 whole garlic bulb
2 bay leaves
5ml/1 tsp black peppercorns, lightly crushed
250g/9oz/1¼ cups dried chickpeas, soaked
   overnight and drained

2 quarters corn-fed chicken
1 small onion, studded with 2 or 3 cloves
2 large carrots, cut into big pieces
2 leeks, cut into chunks
500g/1¼lb small new potatoes, scrubbed
2 red chorizo sausages
1 *morcilla* or 250g/9oz black pudding
   (blood sausage)
30ml/2 tbsp long grain rice
1 small (bell) pepper, finely diced
salt

1 Put the salt meat – brisket or silverside, bacon or pork and knuckle – into a large pan and cover with water. Bring slowly to the boil, simmer for 5 minutes to remove excess salt, and drain.

2 Using a very large stockpot (with a capacity of at least 6 litres/10 pints/5 quarts), pack in all the meat, skinside down, with the marrowbone and trotter. Add the garlic bulb, bay leaves and peppercorns, with water to cover. Bring to simmering point, skimming off any scum, with a slotted spoon.

3 Add the drained chickpeas, cover and simmer on the lowest possible heat for 1½ hours, checking occasionally that there is enough liquid. Add the chicken and onion to the pot. Cook until the chickpeas are done.

4 Start the vegetables. Put the carrots, leeks and potatoes into a large pan with the chorizo (but not the *morcilla* or black pudding). Cover with water and bring to the boil. Simmer for 25 minutes, until the potatoes are cooked. About 5 minutes before the end, add the *morcilla* or black pudding.

5 Strain off enough broth from the meat pot (about 1.2 litres/2 pints/5 cups) into a pan, for soup. Bring back to the boil, sprinkle in the rice and cook for 15 minutes. Add the diced pepper and cook for 2–3 minutes more. Serve the soup as the first course.

6 Drain the vegetables and sausages and arrange on a platter. Serve as a separate second course or as an accompaniment with the meat.

7 Slice the meats, removing the marrow from the bone and adding it to the chickpeas. Arrange with all the meats on a heated serving platter, moistening with a little broth.

Nutritional information per portion: Energy 593kcal/2478kJ; Protein 46.4g; Carbohydrate 37g, of which sugars 4.5g; Fat 29.6g, of which saturates 10.1g; Cholesterol 138mg; Calcium 116mg; Fibre 5.3g; Sodium 1100mg.

Lamb with red peppers and Rioja

World-famous for its red wine, Rioja also produces excellent red peppers. It even has a red pepper fair, at Lodoso, every year. Together they give this lamb stew a lovely rich flavour. Boiled potatoes make a very good accompaniment.

SERVES 4

15ml/1 tbsp plain (all-purpose) flour
1kg/2¼lb lean lamb, cubed
60ml/4 tbsp olive oil
2 red onions, sliced
4 garlic cloves, sliced
10ml/2 tsp paprika
1.5ml/¼ tsp ground cloves
400ml/14fl oz/1²/₃ cups red Rioja
150ml/¼ pint/²/₃ cup lamb stock
2 bay leaves
2 thyme sprigs
3 red (bell) peppers, halved and seeded
salt and ground black pepper
bay leaves and thyme sprigs, to garnish
    (optional)

1 Preheat the oven to 160°C/ 325°F/Gas 3. Season the flour, add the lamb and toss lightly to coat.

2 Heat the oil in a pan and fry the lamb until browned. Transfer to an ovenproof dish. Fry the onions and garlic until soft. Add to the meat.

3 Add the paprika, cloves, Rioja, lamb stock, bay leaves and thyme and then bring the mixture to a gentle simmer.

4 Add the halved and seeded red peppers. Cover the dish with a lid or foil and cook for about 30 minutes, or until the meat is tender.

5 Check the seasoning. Garnish with more bay leaves and thyme sprigs, if you like.

Nutritional information per portion: Energy 635kcal/2646kJ; Protein 49.8g; Carbohydrate 4.1g, of which sugars 0.4g; Fat 39.4g, of which saturates 14.6g; Cholesterol 190mg; Calcium 37mg; Fibre 0.2g; Sodium 223mg.

Veal casserole with broad beans

This delicate stew, flavoured with sherry and plenty of garlic, is a spring dish made with new vegetables – menestra de ternera. For a delicious flavour be sure to add plenty of parsley just before serving. Lamb is equally good cooked in this way.

SERVES 6

45ml/3 tbsp olive oil

1.3–1.6kg/3–3¹/₂lb veal, cut into
    5cm/2in cubes

1 large onion, chopped

6 large garlic cloves, unpeeled

1 bay leaf

5ml/1 tsp paprika

240ml/8fl oz/1 cup fino sherry

100g/4oz/scant 1 cup shelled, skinned
    broad (fava) beans

60ml/4 tbsp chopped fresh flat
    leaf parsley

salt and ground black pepper

1 Heat 30ml/2 tbsp oil in a large, heavy pan. Add half the meat and brown well on all sides. Transfer to a plate. Brown the rest of the meat and remove from the pan.

2 Add the remaining oil to the pan and cook the onion until soft. Return the meat and stir well to mix with the onion.

3 Add the garlic cloves, bay leaf, paprika and sherry. Season with salt and black pepper. Cover and cook very gently for 30–40 minutes.

4 Add the broad beans to the pan about 10 minutes before the end of the cooking time. Check the seasoning and stir in the chopped parsley just before serving.

Nutritional information per portion: Energy 352kcal/1473kJ; Protein 47.4g; Carbohydrate 3.6g, of which sugars 1.3g; Fat 11.6g, of which saturates 2.8g; Cholesterol 182mg; Calcium 34mg; Fibre 1.2g; Sodium 244mg.

Lamb cochifrito

Aragon and Navarre in the Pyrenees are known for their fine ingredients – and also for their simple cooking.

SERVES 4

800g/1¾lb very well-trimmed, tender lamb, in cubes or strips
30ml/2 tbsp olive oil, plus extra
1 onion, chopped
2 garlic cloves, finely chopped
5ml/1 tsp paprika
juice of 2 lemons
15ml/1 tbsp finely chopped fresh parsley
salt and ground black pepper

1 Season the lamb with salt and ground black pepper. Heat the 30ml/2 tbsp olive oil in a large frying pan over a high heat and add the meat in handfuls. Add the onion at the same time, and keep pushing the meat around the pan. Add more meat to the pan as each batch is sealed. Add the chopped garlic and a little more oil if necessary.

2 When the meat is golden and the onion soft, sprinkle with paprika and lemon juice. Cover and simmer for 15 minutes. Check the seasonings and sprinkle with the parsley, then serve.

Nutritional information per portion: Energy 424kcal/1766kJ; Protein 40.1g; Carbohydrate 2.3g, of which sugars 1.1g; Fat 28.4g, of which saturates 11.2g; Cholesterol 152mg; Calcium 44mg; Fibre 0.7g; Sodium 177mg.

Skewered lamb with red onion salsa

The Moors first introduced skewered and barbecued meat to Spain, where it has been popular for over 1,500 years.

SERVES 4

500–675g/1¼–1½lb ready-trimmed, cubed lamb
5ml/1 tsp ground cumin
10ml/2 tsp paprika
30ml/2 tbsp olive oil
salt and ground black pepper

FOR THE RED ONION SALSA
1 red onion, very thinly sliced
1 large tomato, seeded and chopped
15ml/1 tbsp red wine vinegar
3–4 fresh basil or mint leaves, roughly torn

1 Season the lamb with the cumin, paprika, oil and black pepper. Toss well to coat. Leave in a refrigerator overnight. Then, spear the cubes of lamb on four skewers, leaving one end of each of the skewers free for picking up.

2 To make the salsa, put the onion, tomato, vinegar and basil or mint in a small bowl and mix. Season to taste.

3 Cook on a barbecue or preheat the grill (broiler) with the shelf about 15cm/6in from the heat. Generously brush the grill pan with oil.

4 Season the lamb with salt and cook for 5–10 minutes, turning the skewers, until the lamb is well browned but still slightly pink in the centre. Serve hot, with the salsa.

Nutritional information per portion: Energy 294kcal/1224kJ; Protein 25.4g; Carbohydrate 3.3g, of which sugars 1.6g; Fat 20.1g, of which saturates 7.4g; Cholesterol 95mg; Calcium 22mg; Fibre 0.5g; Sodium 112mg.

Solomillo with Cabrales sauce

Well-hung beef is a feature of the Basque country, served here with Cabrales, the blue cheese from Spain's northern mountains. French Roquefort is also extremely popular.

SERVES 4

25g/1oz/2 tbsp butter
30ml/2 tbsp olive oil
4 fillet steaks, cut 5cm/2in thick, about
    150g/5oz each
salt and coarsely ground black pepper
fresh flat leaf parsley, to garnish

FOR THE BLUE CHEESE SAUCE

30ml/2 tbsp Spanish brandy
150ml/5fl oz/²/₃ cup double (heavy)
    cream
75g/3oz Cabrales or Roquefort cheese,
    crumbled

1 Heat the butter and oil together in a heavy frying pan, over a high heat. Season the steaks well. Fry them for 2 minutes on each side, to sear them.

2 Lower the heat slightly and cook for a further 2–3 minutes on each side, or according to your taste. Remove the steaks to a warm plate.

3 To make the sauce, reduce the heat and add the brandy, stirring to pick up the juices. Add the cream and boil to reduce a little.

4 Add the crumbled cheese and mash it into the sauce using a spoon. Taste for seasoning. Serve in a small sauce jug (pitcher), or poured over the steaks. Garnish the beef with parsley.

Nutritional information per portion: Energy 573kcal/2374kJ; Protein 36.3g; Carbohydrate 0.7g, of which sugars 0.7g; Fat 45.4g, of which saturates 24.4g; Cholesterol 170mg; Calcium 117mg; Fibre 0g; Sodium 341mg.

Rabo de toro

In the Spanish kitchen, the most famous part of the bull is his tail — although most people are more likely to cook with oxtail. This stew can be prepared several days ahead.

SERVES 6

60ml/4 tbsp olive oil

2 onions, chopped

1.6kg/3¹/₂lb oxtail, chopped across

30ml/2 tbsp plain (all-purpose) flour,
    seasoned with salt, paprika and pepper

6 carrots, cut into short lengths

2 large garlic cloves, smashed

1 bay leaf

2 thyme sprigs

2 leeks, thinly sliced

1 clove

pinch of freshly grated nutmeg

350ml/12fl oz/1¹/₂ cups red wine

30ml/2 tbsp vinegar

350ml/12fl oz/1¹/₂ cups stock

30ml/2 tbsp fino sherry

60ml/4 tbsp chopped fresh parsley

salt, paprika and black pepper

boiled potatoes, to serve

1 Preheat the oven to 150°C/300°F/Gas 2. Heat 30ml/2 tbsp oil in a large frying pan, add the onions and fry until softened. Remove to a casserole.

2 Dust the oxtail pieces all over with the seasoned flour. Add the remaining oil to the pan and put in the the oxtail pieces. Fry, turning them to brown all over, then fit into the casserole, standing upright in a single layer.

3 Push the carrots into the spaces between the pieces of oxtail. Tuck in the garlic cloves, bay leaf and thyme sprigs and add the leeks. Add the clove, grated nutmeg and more black pepper. Pour in the wine, vinegar and enough stock to cover. Bring to simmering point, then cover the casserole with a lid. Cook in the oven for about 3 hours, or until the meat is falling off the bones.

4 Skim the fat off the top of the stew. Spoon the larger meat pieces on to a plate and remove the bones and fat. Push all the remaining oxtail and carrots to one end of the pan and discard the bay leaf and thyme. Spoon the garlic and some of the soft vegetables into a food processor and purée with the sherry. Return the meat and purée to the casserole and heat through. Stir in the parsley, check the seasonings and serve with boiled potatoes.

Nutritional information per portion: Energy 392kcal/1638kJ; Protein 32.1g; Carbohydrate 8.1g, of which sugars 4g; Fat 21.1g, of which saturates 1.1g; Cholesterol 0mg; Calcium 39mg; Fibre 1g; Sodium 199mg.

Ropa vieja

The name of this dish means "old clothes", which sounds much more romantic than leftovers. It is a dish for using up meats from the cocido, and the recipe shows both Jewish and Arab influences.

SERVES 4

2 small aubergines (eggplants), cubed
90ml/6 tbsp olive oil
1 large onion, chopped
3 garlic cloves, finely chopped
1 fresh, or baked, red (bell) pepper,
    seeded and sliced (optional)
400g/14oz can tomatoes
250ml/8fl oz/1 cup meat stock
2.5ml/1/2 tsp ground allspice
2.5ml/1/2 tsp ground cumin
pinch of ground cloves
2.5ml/1/2 tsp cayenne pepper
400g/14oz cooked beef, cubed, or mixed
    turkey, ham, etc
400g/14oz can chickpeas, drained
salt and ground black pepper
chopped fresh mint, to garnish (optional)

1 Put the aubergine cubes into a colander. Sprinkle with 10ml/2 tsp salt, turning the cubes over. Leave to drain for 1 hour. Rinse, then squeeze them dry using kitchen paper.

2 Meanwhile put 30ml/2 tbsp oil in a large, heavy pan and fry the onion and garlic until soft. If using a fresh pepper, add it to the pan and stir-fry until softened.

3 Add the tomatoes, stock, allspice, cumin, cloves, cayenne and the baked pepper, if using. Season to taste. Add the meat and simmer.

4 Heat 45ml/3 tbsp oil over a high heat in a frying pan. Fry the aubergine cubes until they are brown on all sides.

5 Add the aubergine and chickpeas to the large pan and bring to a simmer, adding a little more stock to cover – the dish should be almost solid. Check the seasonings, garnish with mint, if using, and serve.

Nutritional information per portion: Energy 486kcal/2029kJ; Protein 31.9g; Carbohydrate 24.8g, of which sugars 8.5g; Fat 29.5g, of which saturates 6.7g; Cholesterol 58mg; Calcium 70mg; Fibre 7.5g; Sodium 297mg.

Rabbit salmorejo

The Carthaginians and Romans named Spain "Rabbit Land". The modern name, España, *is derived from the Latin* Hispania *and reminds us how common rabbits, and rabbit dishes, are in Spain.*

SERVES 4

675g/1½lb rabbit, jointed
300ml/½ pint/1¼ cups dry white wine
15ml/1 tbsp sherry vinegar
several oregano sprigs
2 bay leaves
30ml/2 tbsp plain (all-purpose) flour
90ml/6 tbsp olive oil
175g/6oz baby (pearl) onions, peeled and
   left whole
4 garlic cloves, sliced
150ml/¼ pint/⅔ cup chicken stock
1 dried chilli, seeded and finely chopped
10ml/2 tsp paprika
salt and ground black pepper
fresh flat leaf parsley sprigs, to garnish
   (optional)

1 Put the rabbit in a bowl. Add the wine, vinegar, oregano and bay leaves and toss together. Marinate for several hours or overnight in the refrigerator.

2 Drain the rabbit, reserving the marinade, and pat it dry with kitchen paper. Season the flour and use to dust the marinated rabbit.

3 Heat the oil in a large, wide flameproof casserole or frying pan. Fry the rabbit pieces until golden on all sides, then remove them and set aside. Fry the onions until they are beginning to colour, then reserve on a separate plate.

4 Add the garlic to the pan and fry, then add the strained marinade, with the chicken stock, chilli and paprika.

5 Return the rabbit and the reserved onions to the pan. Bring to a simmer, then cover and simmer gently for about 45 minutes until the rabbit is tender. Check the seasoning, adding more vinegar and paprika if necessary. Serve the dish garnished with a few sprigs of flat leaf parsley, if you like.

Nutritional information per portion: Energy 311kcal/1294kJ; Protein 23.2g; Carbohydrate 9.5g, of which sugars 2.6g; Fat 20.4g, of which saturates 4.1g; Cholesterol 83mg; Calcium 65mg; Fibre 0.9g; Sodium 52mg.

Carne con chocolate

Chocolate came to Europe via Spain. It is not naturally sweet and so chocolate squares are used in Spain in the way that other countries use gravy browning. It gives this stew a rich darkness.

SERVES 6

60ml/4 tbsp olive oil
1kg/2¼lb trimmed stewing beef
5ml/1 tsp paprika
150g/5oz smoked bacon lardons, or pancetta
1 large Spanish (Bermuda) onion, chopped
4 carrots, thickly sliced
1 large leek, white only, sliced
6 garlic cloves, crushed
225g/8oz brown cap (cremini) mushrooms, sliced
4 tomatoes, peeled, seeded and chopped
45ml/3 tbsp plain (all-purpose) flour

12 peppercorns, crushed
1 pig's trotter (foot), sawn through
250ml/8fl oz/1 cup dry red wine
1 bay leaf
4 sprigs of thyme
120ml/4fl oz/½ cup Spanish brandy
300ml/10fl oz/1¼ cups meat stock
450g/1lb small potatoes, peeled
25g/1oz dark (bittersweet) chocolate, grated
salt and ground black pepper
45ml/3 tbsp chopped fresh parsley, to garnish

1 Preheat the oven to 180°C/350°F/Gas 4. Heat 30ml/2 tbsp oil in a frying pan. Season the beef with paprika and fry in two batches, over a high heat, turning until browned on all sides. Reserve the first batch on a plate when done. Add a little more oil and fry the second batch.

2 Meanwhile heat 15ml/1 tbsp oil in a large flameproof casserole and fry the bacon or pancetta. When the fat starts to run, add the onion, carrots and leek and cook gently until the onion softens.

3 Add the garlic to the pan, together with the mushrooms and tomatoes. Stir and cook gently, then sprinkle with the flour and cook briefly.

4 Add the meat, peppercorns and salt to the casserole. Tuck in the trotter. Add a little wine, stir to deglaze, then add all the wine, stirring. Add the bay leaf and thyme. Pour in brandy and stock to cover. Return to a simmer, then cover and cook in the oven for 1¼ hours.

5 Cook the potatoes in a pan of boiling water for 15 minutes. Add them to the casserole with the chocolate. Simmer for 30 minutes. Remove the trotter and serve, sprinkled with parsley.

Nutritional information per portion: Energy 648kcal/2705kJ; Protein 46.1g; Carbohydrate 29.8g, of which sugars 12.1g; Fat 31g, of which saturates 10.4g; Cholesterol 113mg; Calcium 62mg; Fibre 4.6g; Sodium 459mg.

Venison chops with romesco sauce

Romesco *is the Catalan word for the* ñora *chilli. It lends a spicy roundness to one of Spain's greatest sauces. It can be served cold as a dip, but this version is the ideal partner for game chops.*

SERVES 4

4 venison chops, cut 2cm/³⁄₄in thick and
    about 175–200g/6–7oz each
30ml/2 tbsp olive oil
50g/2oz/4 tbsp butter
braised Savoy cabbage, to serve

FOR THE SAUCE
3 *ñora* chillies
1 hot dried chilli

25g/1oz/¹⁄₄ cup almonds
150ml/¹⁄₄ pint/²⁄₃ cup olive oil
1 slice stale bread, crusts removed
3 garlic cloves, chopped
3 tomatoes, peeled, seeded and
    roughly chopped
60ml/4 tbsp sherry vinegar
60ml/4 tbsp red wine vinegar
salt and ground black pepper

1 To make the romesco sauce, slit the chillies and remove the seeds, then leave the chillies to soak in warm water for 30 minutes until soft. Drain the chillies, dry them on kitchen paper and chop finely.

2 Dry-fry the almonds in a frying pan over a medium heat, shaking the pan occasionally, until the nuts are toasted evenly. Transfer the nuts to a food processor or blender.

3 Add 45ml/3 tbsp oil to the pan and fry the bread slice until golden on both sides. Lift it out with a slotted spoon and drain on kitchen paper. Tear the bread and add to the food processor or blender. Fry the garlic in the remaining oil.

4 Add the soaked chillies and tomatoes to the processor or blender. Tip in the garlic, with the oil from the pan and blend the mixture to form a smooth paste. With the motor running, gradually add the remaining olive oil and then the sherry and wine vinegars. When the sauce is smooth, scrape it into a bowl and season to taste. Cover with clear film (plastic wrap) and chill for 2 hours.

5 Season the chops with pepper. Heat the olive oil and butter in a heavy frying pan and fry the chops for about 5 minutes each side until golden brown and cooked through. When the chops are almost cooked, transfer the sauce to a pan and heat it gently. If it is too thick, stir in a little boiling water. Serve the sauce with the chops, accompanied by braised cabbage.

Nutritional information per portion: Energy 415kcal/1741kJ; Protein 46.9g; Carbohydrate 6.2g, of which sugars 2.9g; Fat 24g, of which saturates 9.3g; Cholesterol 127mg; Calcium 40mg; Fibre 1.3g; Sodium 229mg.

Desserts
and baking

Iced desserts were introduced to Spain

by the Moors, who also created luxurious

dishes of fruit in syrups. Caramel is a

much-loved flavour and is used in a winter

fruit salad of oranges and a "drunken"

cake soaked in brandy. As well as desserts

this chapter has delicious pastries and

cookies, breakfast rolls and satisfying,

solid loaves.

Honey-baked figs with hazelnut ice cream

Two wild ingredients – figs and hazelnuts – are used to make this delectable dessert, higos con helado de avellana. *Fresh figs are baked in a lightly spiced lemon and honey syrup and are served with home-made roasted hazelnut ice cream.*

SERVES 4

finely pared rind of 1 lemon
1 cinnamon stick, roughly broken
60ml/4 tbsp clear honey
8 large figs

FOR THE HAZELNUT ICE CREAM

450ml/¾ pint/scant 2 cups double
    (heavy) cream
50g/2oz/¼ cup caster (superfine) sugar
3 large (US extra large) egg yolks
1.5ml/¼ tsp vanilla extract
75g/3oz/¾ cup hazelnuts

1 Make the ice cream. Gently heat the cream in a pan until almost boiling. Meanwhile, beat the sugar and egg yolks in a bowl until creamy.

2 Pour a little hot cream into the egg yolk mixture and stir with a wooden spoon. Pour back into the pan and mix well. Cook over a low heat, stirring constantly, until the mixture thickens slightly and lightly coats the back of the spoon – do not allow it to boil.

3 Pour the custard into a bowl, stir in the vanilla extract and leave to cool.

4 Preheat the oven to 180°C/350°F/Gas 4. Place the hazelnuts on a baking sheet and roast for 10–12 minutes, or until golden. Leave the nuts to cool, then grind them in a food processor.

5 If you have an ice cream machine, pour in the cold custard and churn until half set. Add the ground hazelnuts and continue to churn until the ice cream is thick. Freeze until firm.

6 Working by hand, pour the custard into a freezerproof container and freeze for 2 hours, or until the custard feels firm around the edges. Turn into a bowl and beat with an electric whisk or turn into a food processor and beat until smooth. Stir in the hazelnuts and freeze until half set. Beat once more, then freeze until firm.

7 Preheat the oven to 200°C/400°F/Gas 6. Remove the ice cream from the freezer and allow to soften slightly.

8 To make the syrup, put the lemon rind, cinnamon stick, honey and 200ml/7fl oz/scant 1 cup water in a small pan and heat slowly until boiling. Simmer the mixture for 5 minutes, then leave to stand for 15 minutes.

9 Using a sharp knife, cut the figs almost into quarters but leaving the figs still attached at the base. Pack them into a casserole, in a single layer, and pour the honey syrup round and over them. Cover the dish tightly with foil and bake for 10 minutes.

10 Arrange the figs on small serving plates, with the cooking syrup poured round them. Serve accompanied by a scoop or two of the ice cream.

Nutritional information per portion: Energy 917kcal/3805kJ; Protein 8.3g; Carbohydrate 50.5g, of which sugars 50.1g; Fat 77.2g, of which saturates 39.7g; Cholesterol 311mg; Calcium 207mg; Fibre 4.2g; Sodium 60mg.

Rum and raisin ice cream

Helado con ron y pasas *is an ice cream with a long tradition in Spain. Dark rum comes from the former Spanish island of Cuba, while the Malaga region produces huge, black Muscatel raisins.*

SERVES 4–6

150g/5oz/1 cup large Muscatel raisins, Malagan if possible
60ml/4 tbsp dark rum
4 egg yolks
75g/3oz/6 tbsp light brown sugar
5ml/1 tsp cornflour (cornstarch)
300ml/½ pint/1¼ cups full-fat (whole) milk
300ml/½ pint/1¼ cups whipping cream
wafers or biscuits (cookies), to serve

1 Put the raisins in a bowl, add the rum and mix well. Cover and leave to soak for 3–4 hours or overnight.

2 Whisk together the egg yolks, sugar and cornflour in a bowl until thick and foamy. Heat the milk in a pan to just below boiling point.

3 Whisk the milk into the eggs, then pour back into the pan. Cook over a gentle heat, stirring with a wooden spoon, until the custard thickens and is smooth. Leave to cool.

4 Whip the cream until it is just thick, then fold it into the custard. Working by hand, pour the mixture into a freezerproof container. Freeze for 4 hours, beating once in a food processor after 2 hours, then beat again after 4 hours.

5 Fold the soaked raisins into the ice cream, then cover and freeze for 2–3 hours, or until it is firm enough to scoop. Serve the ice cream in bowls or tall glasses, with wafers or dessert biscuits.

Nutritional information per portion: Energy 397kcal/1654kJ; Protein 5.2g; Carbohydrate 34.9g, of which sugars 34.1g; Fat 24.8g, of which saturates 14.2g; Cholesterol 190mg; Calcium 123mg; Fibre 0.5g; Sodium 56mg.

Sorbete de limón

The Moors introduced ices to Andalucia a thousand years ago. Eating this smooth, tangy sorbet, you can imagine yourself in a palace like the one at Granada, lounging on silken cushions.

SERVES 6

200g/7oz/1 cup caster (superfine) sugar
300ml/¼ pint/1¼ cups water
4 lemons, washed
1 large (US extra large) egg white
a little sugar, for sprinkling

1 Put the sugar and water into a heavy pan and bring slowly to the boil, stirring occasionally, until the sugar has just dissolved.

2 Pare the rind from two of the lemons directly into the pan. Simmer for 2 minutes without stirring, then remove from the heat. Leave the syrup to cool, then chill.

3 Squeeze the juice from all the lemons and strain it into the syrup, making sure all the pips (seeds) are removed. Take the rind out of the syrup and set it aside for the garnish.

4 Working by hand, strain the syrup into a plastic tub or a similar shallow freezerproof container and freeze for 4 hours, until the mixture is mushy.

5 Scoop the mixture into a food processor and beat until smooth. Whisk the egg white with a fork until it is just frothy. Spoon the sorbet back into its container and beat in the egg white. Freeze for 1 hour.

6 To make the garnish, cut the rind into strips and sprinkle with sugar. Scoop the sorbet into bowls and decorate with sugared lemon rind.

Nutritional information per portion: Energy 135kcal/574kJ; Protein 0.7g; Carbohydrate 35.1g, of which sugars 35.1g; Fat 0g, of which saturates 0g; Cholesterol 0mg; Calcium 19mg; Fibre 0g; Sodium 12mg.

Bitter chocolate mousses

The Spanish introduced chocolate to Europe, and chocolate mousse remains a favourite dessert. These lovely cremas de chocolate *are rich with chocolate, with a hint of orange from the liqueur.*

SERVES 8

225g/8oz dark (bittersweet) chocolate, chopped
30ml/2 tbsp orange liqueur or a good Spanish brandy such as Torres
50g/2oz/¼ cup unsalted (sweet) butter, cut into small pieces
4 large (US extra large) eggs, separated
90ml/6 tbsp whipping cream
45ml/3 tbsp caster (superfine) sugar

1 Place the chocolate and 60ml/4 tbsp water in a pan. Melt over a low heat, stirring. Off the heat whisk in the liqueur or brandy and butter. Beat the egg yolks until thick and creamy, then slowly beat into the chocolate until blended.

2 Whip the cream until soft peaks form, then stir a spoonful into the chocolate mixture to lighten it. Gently fold in the remaining whipped cream.

3 In a clean, grease-free bowl, use an electric mixer to slowly whisk the egg whites until frothy. Increase the speed and continue until the egg whites form soft peaks. Gradually sprinkle the sugar over the egg whites and continue beating until the whites are stiff and glossy.

4 Stir a quarter of the egg whites into the chocolate mixture to lighten it, then gently fold in the remaining whites, cutting down to the bottom of the bowl, along the sides and up to the top in a semicircular motion until they are just combined. Gently spoon the mixture into eight individual dishes or a 2 litre/3½ pint/8 cup bowl. Chill for at least 2 hours until set before serving.

Nutritional information per portion: Energy 300kcal/1251kJ; Protein 4.8g; Carbohydrate 24.1g, of which sugars 23.8g; Fat 20.3g, of which saturates 11.6g; Cholesterol 122mg; Calcium 34mg; Fibre 0.7g; Sodium 78mg.

Crema Catalana

This fabulous dessert of creamy custard topped with a net of brittle sugar may be the origin of all crème brûlées. **Cremat** *is the Catalan word for "burnt", and was probably part of the original name.*

SERVES 4

475ml/16fl oz/2 cups milk
pared rind of ¹/₂ lemon
1 cinnamon stick
4 large (US extra large) egg yolks
105ml/7 tbsp caster (superfine) sugar
25ml/1¹/₂ tbsp cornflour (cornstarch)
ground nutmeg, for sprinkling

1 Put the milk in a pan with the lemon rind and cinnamon stick. Bring to the boil, then simmer for 10 minutes. Remove the lemon rind and cinnamon. Put the egg yolks and 45ml/3 tbsp sugar in a bowl, and whisk until pale yellow. Add the cornflour and mix well.

2 Stir a few tablespoons of the hot milk into the egg yolk mixture, then tip back into the remaining milk. Return to the heat and cook gently, stirring, for about 5 minutes, until thickened and smooth. Do not boil.

3 Pour the custard into four shallow ovenproof dishes, about 13cm/5in in diameter. Once cool, chill for a few hours, or overnight, until firm.

4 No more than 30 minutes before serving, sprinkle each dessert with 15ml/ 1 tbsp of the sugar and a little nutmeg. Preheat the grill (broiler) to high. Place the dishes under the grill, on the highest shelf, and cook for a few seconds until the sugar has caramelized. Remove the custards and leave to cool for a few minutes before serving.

Nutritional information per portion: Energy 244kcal/1030kJ; Protein 7.2g; Carbohydrate 38.8g, of which sugars 33g; Fat 7.8g, of which saturates 2.9g; Cholesterol 217mg; Calcium 182mg; Fibre 0g; Sodium 65mg.

Arrope

This is an old Arab recipe whose name means "syrup"; this version comes from the Pyrenees. Arrope starts as a lovely fruit compote and ends up as a syrupy jam, to be scooped up with bread.

SERVES 10

3 firm peaches, unpeeled
1kg/2¼lb/5 cups sugar
3 large eating apples
finely grated rind of 1 lemon
3 firm pears
finely grated rind of 1 orange

1 small sweet potato, 150g/5oz
    prepared weight
200g/7oz butternut squash, peeled and
    prepared weight
250ml/8fl oz/1 cup dark rum
30ml/2 tbsp clear honey

1 Cut the peaches into eighths, without peeling them, and place in the bottom of a large, heavy pan. Sprinkle with 15ml/1 tbsp of the sugar. Peel and core the apples and cut them into 16 segments, then arrange on top of the peaches. Sprinkle the lemon rind over the top, along with 15ml/1 tbsp of the sugar. Prepare the pears in the same way as the apples, place in the pan, then sprinkle over the orange rind, followed by 15ml/1 tbsp of the sugar.

2 Slice the sweet potato into pieces half the size of the pears and spread them over the top. Prepare the squash in the same way, layering it on top. Sprinkle about 15ml/1 tbsp of the sugar. Cover with a plate that fits inside the rim, and weigh down with a couple of cans. Stand for a minimum of 2 to 12 hours for juice to form.

3 Remove the cans and plate, put the pan over a fairly low heat and bring to a simmer. Cook and soften the fruit for 20 minutes, stirring once or twice to prevent sticking.

4 Add the remaining sugar, in batches, stirring to dissolve each batch before adding the next. Bring the mixture up to a rolling boil, over a medium high heat, and boil very steadily for 45 minutes. Stir and lift off any scum. The syrup should be considerably reduced. Test by pouring a spoonful on a plate. It should wrinkle when a spoon is pulled across.

5 Off the heat, add the rum and honey and stir well to combine. Return the pan to a moderate heat and cook for a further 10 minutes, stirring to prevent the fruit sticking. Remove the pan from the heat and set aside to cool. If the resulting compote is too stiff, stir in some more rum before serving.

Nutritional information per portion: Energy 516kcal/2194kJ; Protein 1.4g; Carbohydrate 120.8g, of which sugars 118.3g; Fat 0.2g, of which saturates 0g; Cholesterol 0mg; Calcium 71mg; Fibre 2.6g; Sodium 15mg.

Hazelnut meringues with nectarines

Meringues go back to Moorish times and hazelnuts are a popular flavouring. Here they are served with cream whipped with Malaga's dessert wine, and stuffed with fresh nectarines.

SERVES 5

3 large (US extra large) egg whites

175g/6oz/generous ³/4 cup caster (superfine) sugar

50g/2oz/¹/2 cup chopped hazelnuts, toasted

300ml/¹/2 pint/1¹/4 cups double (heavy) cream

60ml/4 tbsp sweet Malaga dessert wine

2 nectarines, stoned (pitted) and sliced

fresh mint sprigs, to decorate

1 Preheat the oven to 140°C/275°F/Gas 1. Line two large baking sheets with baking parchment.

2 Whisk the egg whites in a grease-free bowl until they form stiff peaks. Gradually whisk in the sugar a spoonful at a time, until a stiff, glossy meringue forms. Fold two-thirds of the hazelnuts into the egg whites.

3 Divide the meringue mixture between the baking sheets, spooning five ovals on to each one. Sprinkle the remaining hazelnuts over the meringues on one baking sheet, then flatten the tops of the others using the back of a spoon.

4 Bake the meringues for 1–1¹/4 hours until crisp and dry, then lift them off the baking parchment and leave to cool.

5 Put the cream and dessert wine in a bowl and whisk to form soft peaks. Spoon a little of the cream on to each of the plain meringues. Arrange a few nectarine slices on each. Put one cream-topped meringue and one nut-topped meringue on each plate. Garnish with fresh mint and serve immediately.

Nutritional information per portion: Energy 539kcal/2247kJ; Protein 5g; Carbohydrate 43.6g, of which sugars 43.4g; Fat 38.6g, of which saturates 20.5g; Cholesterol 82mg; Calcium 68mg; Fibre 1.3g; Sodium 54mg.

Oranges with caramel wigs

Naranjas con pelucas is a pretty variation on the normal orange salad. The caramelized rind and syrup has a wonderful flavour that contrasts with the oranges.

SERVES 6

6 oranges
120g/4oz/generous ¹/₂ cup caster
    (superfine) sugar
120ml/4fl oz/¹/₂ cup boiling water
cocktail sticks (toothpicks)

1 Thinly pare 12 long strips of orange rind. Peel all the oranges, reserving the rind and discarding the pith. Reserve the juice and freeze the oranges separately for 30 minutes.

2 Slice the oranges horizontally, reform and secure with a cocktail stick. Chill.

3 To make the wigs, simmer the rind for about 5 minutes, drain, rinse, and then repeat. Trim with scissors.

4 Put half the sugar into a pan with 15ml/1 tbsp water. Heat gently until the mixture caramelizes. When it colours, dip the pan into cold water. Add 30ml/2 tbsp hot water and the rind. Stir until the caramel dissolves. Cool the rind.

5 Make a caramel syrup for serving as before. When it has coloured, stand back, pour in the boiling water and stir with a wooden spoon to dissolve. Add the reserved juices and pour into a jug (pitcher).

6 To serve, arrange the orange strips on top of each orange. Remove the cocktail sticks and pour a little caramel syrup round each orange.

Nutritional information per portion: Energy 122kcal/521kJ; Protein 1.4g; Carbohydrate 30.8g, of which sugars 30.8g; Fat 0.1g, of which saturates 0g; Cholesterol 0mg; Calcium 66mg; Fibre 2g; Sodium 7mg.

Leche frita with black fruit sauce

The name of this dessert means "fried milk", but it is really custard squares. It is very popular in the Basque country, and has a melting, creamy centre and crunchy, golden coating.

SERVES 6–8

550ml/18fl oz/2^1/$_2$ cups full-fat (whole) milk

3 finely pared strips of lemon rind

^{1}/$_2$ cinnamon stick

90g/3^1/$_2$oz/^{1}/$_2$ cup caster (superfine) sugar, plus extra for sprinkling

60ml/4 tbsp cornflour (cornstarch)

30ml/2 tbsp plain (all-purpose) flour

3 large (US extra large) egg yolks

2 large (US extra large) eggs

90–120ml/6–8 tbsp stale breadcrumbs or dried crumbs

sunflower oil, for frying

ground cinnamon, for dusting

FOR THE SAUCE

450g/1lb blackcurrants or blackberries

90g/3^1/$_2$oz/^{1}/$_2$ cup sugar, plus extra for dusting

1 Put the milk, lemon rind, cinnamon stick and sugar in a pan and bring to the boil, stirring gently. Cover and leave to infuse for 20 minutes.

2 Put the cornflour and flour in a bowl and beat in the egg yolks with a wooden spoon. Add a little of the milk and beat to make a smooth batter.

3 Strain the remaining hot milk into the batter, then pour back into the pan. Cook over a low heat, stirring constantly. (The mixture won't curdle, but it will thicken unevenly if you let it.) Cook for a couple of minutes, until it thickens and separates from the side of the pan.

4 Beat the mixture hard with the spoon to ensure a really smooth consistency. Pour into an 18–20cm/7–8in, 1cm/^{1}/$_2$in-deep rectangular dish, and smooth the top. Cool, then chill until firm.

5 Make the fruit sauce. Cook the blackcurrants or blackberries with the sugar and a little water for about 10 minutes until soft.

6 Reserve 30–45ml/2–3 tbsp whole currants or berries, then put the rest in a food processor and blend to make a smooth purée. Return the purée and berries to the pan.

7 Cut the chilled custard into eight or twelve squares. Beat the eggs in a shallow dish and spread out the breadcrumbs on a plate. Lift half of the squares into the egg. Coat on both sides, then lift into the crumbs and cover all over. Repeat with the second batch of squares.

8 Pour about 1cm/$\frac{1}{2}$in oil into a deep frying pan and heat until very hot.

9 Lift two or three coated squares into the oil and fry for a couple of minutes, shaking or spooning the oil over the top, until golden. Reserve on kitchen paper, while frying the other batches.

10 To serve, arrange the custard squares on plates and sprinkle with sugar and cinnamon. Pour a circle of warm sauce round the squares, distributing the whole berries evenly.

COOK'S TIP
In Spain, milk is usually drunk at breakfast or used for cheese. In northern Spain, the milk has a wonderful quality and has been given special status as a dessert ingredient. Most popular of all the milk desserts are leche frita, flan *and* filloas *(thin pancakes).*

Nutritional information per portion: Energy 272kcal/1150kJ; Protein 7.7g; Carbohydrate 48.1g, of which sugars 27.1g; Fat 6.8g, of which saturates 2.7g; Cholesterol 146mg; Calcium 151mg; Fibre 2.2g; Sodium 169mg.

Apple-stuffed crêpes

Spain's dairy country lies along the cooler northern coast and crêpes are extremely popular there. In the Asturias, crêpes are made with a variety of sweet fillings such as this apple one.

SERVES 4

115g/4oz/1 cup plain (all-purpose) flour
pinch of salt
2 large (US extra large) eggs
175ml/6fl oz/³⁄4 cup full-fat (whole) milk
120ml/4fl oz/¹⁄2 cup sweet (hard) cider
butter, for frying
4 eating apples
60ml/4 tbsp caster (superfine) sugar
120ml/8 tbsp clear honey, and 150ml/
**   ¹⁄4 pint/²⁄3 cup double (heavy) cream,**
**   to serve**

1 Make the batter. Sift the flour and salt into a large bowl. Add the eggs and milk and beat until smooth. Stir in the cider. Leave to stand for 30 minutes.

2 Heat a small heavy non-stick frying pan. Add a little butter and ladle in enough batter to coat the pan thinly. Cook the crêpe for about 1 minute until golden underneath, then flip it over and cook the other side until golden. Slide the crêpe on to a plate, then repeat with the remaining batter to make seven more. Set the crêpes aside and keep warm.

3 Make the apple filling. Core the apples and cut them into thick slices. Heat 15g/¹⁄2oz butter in a large frying pan. Add the apples to the pan and cook until golden on both sides. Transfer the slices to a bowl with a slotted spoon and sprinkle with sugar.

4 Fold each pancake in half, then fold in half again to form a cone. Fill each with some of the fried apples. Place two filled pancakes on each dessert plate. Drizzle with a little honey and serve at once, accompanied by cream.

Nutritional information per portion: Energy 489kcal/2057kJ; Protein 8.2g; Carbohydrate 71.5g, of which sugars 49.6g; Fat 20.1g, of which saturates 11.3g; Cholesterol 139mg; Calcium 137mg; Fibre 2.1g; Sodium 69mg.

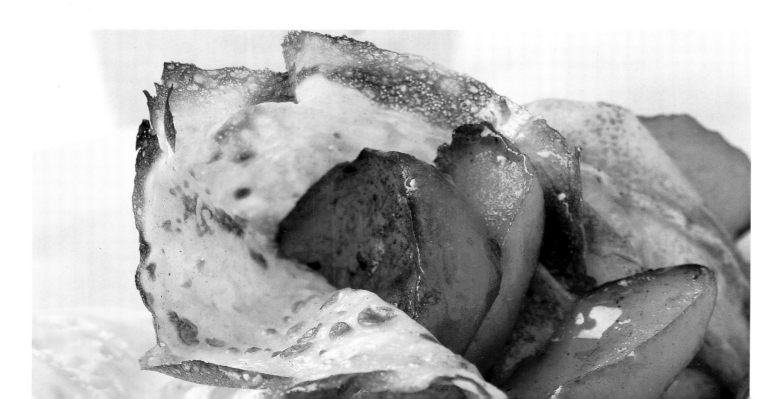

Torrijas

Translated as "poor knights", these sugared toasts are perfect for almost every occasion.
They make a good tea-time snack, or a delicious accompaniment to a cup of hot chocolate.

SERVES 4

120ml/4fl oz/¹/₂ cup white wine
12 thick rounds of stale French bread
2 large eggs
60–90ml/4–6 tbsp sunflower oil
ground cinnamon, and caster (superfine)
 sugar, for dusting

1 Pour the wine into a shallow dish and dip the bread rounds into it. Beat the eggs together in another shallow dish. Dip half the bread rounds into the beaten egg on each side so that they are completely covered.

2 Heat 60ml/4 tbsp oil in a pan until very hot and fry the bread rounds for about 1 minute on each side until crisp and golden. Reserve on kitchen paper, then dip and fry the rest, adding more oil if necessary. Serve hot, sprinkled with cinnamon and sugar.

COOK'S TIP
These toasts are often enjoyed at festivals and are a typical dish from Madrid. Milk can be used in place of white wine, if liked, making them suitable for children.

Nutritional information per portion: Energy 419kcal/1763kJ; Protein 12.2g; Carbohydrate 56.3g, of which sugars 3g; Fat 15.7g, of which saturates 2.4g; Cholesterol 95mg; Calcium 138mg; Fibre 2.4g; Sodium 652mg.

Churros

This Spanish breakfast doughnut is sold in all tapas bars, which so conveniently transform into cafés in the morning. They are also served at festivals, piped into great vats of oil, cut into loops and then tied with grass string to eat as you walk.

MAKES 12–15

200g/7oz/1¾ cups plain
  (all-purpose) flour
1.5ml/¼ tsp salt
30ml/2 tbsp caster (superfine) sugar
250ml/8fl oz/1 cup water

60ml/4 tbsp olive or sunflower oil
1 egg, beaten
caster (superfine) sugar and ground
  cinnamon, for dusting
oil, for deep-frying

1 Sift the flour, salt and sugar on to a plate or piece of baking parchment. Put the water and oil in a pan and bring to the boil.

2 Tip the flour mixture into the pan and beat with a wooden spoon until the mixture forms a stiff paste. Leave to cool for 2 minutes, then gradually beat in the egg to make a smooth dough.

3 Oil a large baking sheet. Sprinkle plenty of sugar on to a plate and stir in a little cinnamon.

4 Spoon the dough into a large piping (pastry) bag fitted with a 1cm/½in plain piping nozzle. Pipe little coils or "S" shapes on to the baking sheet.

5 Heat 5cm/2in of oil in a large pan to 168°C/336°F, or until a little piece of dough dropped into the oil sizzles on the surface.

6 Using an oiled metal spatula, lower several of the piped shapes into the oil and fry for about 2 minutes until light golden.

7 Drain the churros on kitchen paper, then dip them into the sugar and cinnamon mixture, to coat. Cook the remaining churros in the same way and serve immediately.

Nutritional information per churro: Energy 111kcal/464kJ; Protein 1.7g; Carbohydrate 12.5g, of which sugars 2.3g; Fat 6.4g, of which saturates 0.9g; Cholesterol 13mg; Calcium 22mg; Fibre 0.4g; Sodium 5mg.

Biscocho borracho

The name of this dessert translates as "drunken cake", indicating that it is soaked in brandy-flavoured syrup. This version of the recipe is made in a mould, then turned out.

SERVES 6–8

butter, for greasing
90g/3½oz/¾ cup plain
 (all-purpose) flour
6 large (US extra large) eggs
90g/3½oz/½ cup caster
 (superfine) sugar
finely grated rind of 1 lemon

90ml/6 tbsp toasted flaked almonds
250ml/8fl oz/1 cup cream, to serve

FOR THE SYRUP

115g/4oz/½ cup caster (superfine) sugar
120ml/4fl oz/½ cup boiling water
105ml/7 tbsp Spanish brandy

1 Starting 1–2 days ahead, preheat the oven to 200°C/400°F/Gas 6. Butter a shallow pan, about 28 x 18cm/11 x 7in. Line the tin with baking parchment and butter well. Sift the flour a couple of times into a bowl. Separate the eggs, putting the whites into a bowl. Put the yolks in a food processor with the sugar and lemon rind and beat until light. Whisk the whites to soft peaks, then work a little white into the yolk mixture.

2 Dribble two spoonfuls of the yolk mixture across the whites, sift some flour over the top and cut in gently with a large spoon. Fold together in this way until all the egg mixture and flour have been incorporated. Turn the cake mixture into the prepared shallow pan and smooth over. Bake for 12 minutes. Leave the cake to set for 5 minutes, then turn out on to a wire rack. Peel off the paper and leave to cool completely.

3 Make the syrup. Place 50g/2oz/¼ cup sugar into a small pan and add 15ml/1 tbsp water. Heat until it caramelizes. As soon as it colours, dip the base of the pan into a bowl of cold water. Add the remaining sugar and pour in the boiling water. Bring back to a simmer, gently stirring until all the sugar has dissolved. Pour into a jug (pitcher) and add the brandy.

4 Put the cake back into the pan and drizzle half the syrup over it. Choose a 700ml/1½ pint/3 cup capacity mould; cut the cake into scallops with a spoon and layer half into the bottom of it. Sprinkle 30ml/2 tbsp almonds over the top and into the cracks. Top with the remaining cake and nuts. Pour the remaining syrup over the cake, cover with foil and weight down the top. Chill until ready to serve. To serve, turn the cake out on to a dish, sprinkle with almonds and serve with the fresh cream.

Nutritional information per portion: Energy 412kcal/1719kJ; Protein 8.9g; Carbohydrate 37.1g, of which sugars 28.3g; Fat 23.2g, of which saturates 9.6g; Cholesterol 176mg; Calcium 96mg; Fibre 1.2g; Sodium 64mg.

Guirlache

This is an Arab sweetmeat from the Pyrenees, combining toasted nuts and caramel to produce a crisp nut brittle – a forerunner of some familiar chocolate bar fillings. It is less well known than turrón, *the Spanish Christmas nougat, which is made with similar ingredients.*

MAKES ABOUT 24 PIECES

115g/4oz/1 cup almonds, half blanched, half unblanched
115g/4oz/1 cup hazelnuts, half blanched, half unblanched
5ml/1 tsp almond oil or a flavourless oil
200g/7oz/1 cup sugar
15ml/1 tbsp lemon juice

1 Preheat the oven to 150°C/300°F/Gas 2. Sprinkle the nuts on a baking sheet and toast for 30 minutes, shaking the sheet occasionally. The nuts should smell pleasant and have turned brown and be very dry.

2 Coarsely chop the toasted nuts or crush them roughly with a rolling pin. Cover another baking tray with foil and grease it with the oil.

3 Put the sugar in a pile in a small pan and pour the lemon juice round it. Cook over a high heat, shaking the pan, until the sugar turns a coffee colour. (As it cooks, the pile of sugar will melt and collapse into caramel.)

4 Immediately tip in the nuts and stir once, then pour the mixture on to the foil and spread out into a thin, even layer. Leave the mixture to harden.

5 Once set, break up the caramel into pieces and store in an airtight tin.

Nutritional information per piece: Energy 94kcal/395kJ; Protein 1.7g; Carbohydrate 9.3g, of which sugars 9.1g; Fat 5.8g, of which saturates 0.5g; Cholesterol 0mg; Calcium 23mg; Fibre 0.7g; Sodium 1mg.

Panellets

The Catalan name for these nutty festival cakes means "little bread", but they are, in fact, closer to marzipan, with a slightly soft centre that is produced by their secret ingredient – sweet potato. They are made for All Saints' Day, on 1st November, when families take flowers to the graveyards.

MAKES ABOUT 24

115g/4oz sweet potato, diced
butter, for greasing
1 large (US extra large) egg, separated
225g/8oz/2 cups ground almonds
200g/7oz/1 cup caster (superfine) sugar,
    plus extra for sprinkling
finely grated rind of 1 small lemon
7.5ml/1½ tsp vanilla extract
60ml/4 tbsp pine nuts
60ml/4 tbsp pistachio nuts, chopped

1 Cook the sweet potato in a pan of boiling water for 15 minutes, or until soft. Drain and leave to cool.

2 Preheat the oven to 200°C/400°F/ Gas 6. Line one or two baking sheets with foil and grease well with butter.

3 Put the sweet potato in a food processor and process to a smooth purée (paste). Work in the egg yolk, almonds, sugar, lemon rind and vanilla extract to make a soft dough. Transfer the dough to a bowl and chill for 30 minutes.

4 Spoon walnut-sized balls of dough on to the foil, spacing them about 2.5cm/1in apart, then flatten them out slightly. Lightly beat the egg white in a bowl and brush over the cakes. Sprinkle half the cakes with pine nuts, about 5ml/1 tsp each, and half with pistachio nuts. Sprinkle with sugar and bake for 10 minutes, or until lightly browned.

5 Leave to cool on the foil, then lift off and store in an airtight container.

Nutritional information per cake: Energy 130kcal/541kJ; Protein 3.1g; Carbohydrate 10.7g, of which sugars 9.6g; Fat 8.6g, of which saturates 0.8g; Cholesterol 8mg; Calcium 32mg; Fibre 1g; Sodium 20mg.

Pestiños

The Arabs invented all sorts of sweet bites, to eat after the main course or with drinks. Bathed in honey syrup, pestiños *were often deep-fried and known as* dulces de sárten, *which means "sweets from the frying pan". However, you can bake them and they puff beautifully in the oven.*

MAKES ABOUT 30

225g/8oz/2 cups plain (all-purpose)
    flour, plus extra for dusting
60ml/4 tbsp sunflower oil
15ml/1 tbsp aniseed, lightly crushed
45ml/3 tbsp caster (superfine) sugar
250ml/8fl oz/1 cup water

60ml/4 tbsp anisette
3 small (US medium) eggs

FOR THE ANIS SYRUP
60ml/4 tbsp clear honey
60ml/4 tbsp anisette or Ricard

1 Preheat the oven to 190°C/375°F/Gas 5. Sift the flour on to a sheet of baking parchment. Heat the oil in a small pan with the crushed aniseed, until the aniseed releases its aroma. Strain the oil into a larger pan and add the sugar, water and anisette. Heat to a rolling boil.

2 Remove the pan from the heat and add the sifted flour, all in one go. Beat vigorously with a wooden spoon until the mixture leaves the sides of the pan clean. Leave to cool.

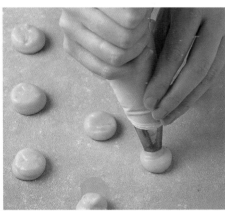

3 Meanwhile lightly beat the eggs. Gradually incorporate the egg into the dough mixture, beating hard. You may not need to use all the egg; the paste should be soft but not sloppy. Reserve any remaining beaten egg.

4 Grease and flour two baking sheets. Fit a plain nozzle to a piping (pastry) bag and pipe small rounds of dough about 2.5cm/1in across on the sheets, spacing them about 2.5cm/1in apart. Brush with the remaining beaten egg. Bake for about 30 minutes, or until lightly brown and an even texture right through. (Lift one off the sheet to test.)

5 Melt the honey in a small pan and stir in the anisette. Just before serving, use a slotted spoon to dunk the pestiños into the syrup.

Nutritional information per bun: Energy 65kcal/272kJ; Protein 1.3g; Carbohydrate 8.9g, of which sugars 3.2g; Fat 2.1g, of which saturates 0.3g; Cholesterol 19mg; Calcium 14mg; Fibre 0.2g; Sodium 8mg.

Twelfth night bread

January 6th, Epiphany, celebrates the arrival of the kings at Christ's manger, and in Spain it is the day for exchanging Christmas gifts. This bread is specially baked for the occasion. Traditionally it contains a bean, a china baby or a coin, and the person to find it is declared king of the party.

SERVES 12

450g/1lb/4 cups unbleached strong
   white bread flour
2.5ml/$\frac{1}{2}$ tsp salt
25g/1oz fresh yeast
140ml/scant $\frac{1}{4}$ pint/scant $\frac{2}{3}$ cup mixed
   lukewarm milk and water
75g/3oz/6 tbsp butter
75g/3oz/6 tbsp caster (superfine) sugar
10ml/2 tsp finely grated lemon rind
10ml/2 tsp finely grated orange rind

2 eggs
15ml/1 tbsp brandy
15ml/1 tbsp orange flower water
silver coin or dried bean (optional)
1 egg white, lightly beaten, for glazing

FOR THE DECORATION
a mixture of glacé (candied) fruit slices
flaked (sliced) almonds

1 Lightly grease a large baking sheet. Sift together the flour and salt into a large bowl. Make a well in the centre.

2 In a bowl, mix the yeast with the milk and water until the yeast has dissolved. Pour into the centre of the flour and stir in enough of the flour from around the sides of the bowl to make a thick batter.

3 Sprinkle a little of the remaining flour over the top of the batter and leave to turn spongy, in a warm place, for about 15 minutes or until frothy.

4 Using an electric whisk or a wooden spoon, beat together the butter and sugar in a bowl until soft and creamy.

5 Add the citrus rinds, eggs, brandy and orange flower water to the flour mixture and mix to a sticky dough.

6 Beat the mixture until it forms a fairly smooth dough. Gradually beat in the butter mixture and beat for a few minutes until the dough is smooth and elastic. Cover with lightly oiled clear film (plastic wrap) and leave to rise, in a warm place, for about 1$\frac{1}{2}$ hours, or until doubled in size.

7 Punch the dough down and turn out on to a lightly floured surface. Gently knead for 2 or 3 minutes, incorporating the lucky coin or bean, if using.

8 Using a rolling pin, roll out the dough into a long strip measuring about 65 x 13cm/26 x 5in.

9 Roll up the dough from one long side like a Swiss roll (jelly roll) to make a long sausage shape. Place seam side down on the prepared baking sheet and seal the ends together. Cover with lightly oiled clear film and leave to rise, in a warm place, for 1–1¹/₂ hours, or until doubled in size.

10 Preheat the oven to 180°C/350°F/Gas 4. Brush the dough ring with lightly beaten egg white and decorate with glacé fruit slices, pushing them slightly into the dough. Sprinkle with flaked almonds and bake for 30–35 minutes, or until risen and golden. Turn out on to a wire rack to cool.

Nutritional information per portion: Energy 217kcal/914kJ; Protein 4.8g; Carbohydrate 36g, of which sugars 7.4g; Fat 6.7g, of which saturates 3.7g; Cholesterol 45mg; Calcium 69mg; Fibre 1.2g; Sodium 54mg.

Pan de cebada

Galicia is known for its country breads, which often include flours other than wheat. A combination of barley and maize flours gives this bread a close, heavy texture and a rich taste.

MAKES 1 LARGE LOAF

cornmeal, for dusting

FOR THE SOURDOUGH STARTER
175g/6oz/1½ cups cornmeal
225g/8oz/2 cups strong wholemeal (whole-wheat) bread flour
75g/3oz/⅔ cup barley flour

FOR THE DOUGH
20g/¾oz fresh yeast
45ml/3 tbsp lukewarm water
225g/8oz/2 cups strong wholemeal bread flour
15ml/1 tbsp salt

1 Make the starter. In a pan, mix the cornmeal with 300ml/½ pint/1¼ cups water, then blend in another 300ml/½ pint/1¼ cups of water. Cook over a gentle heat, stirring, until thickened. Transfer to a large bowl and cool.

2 Put the mixture into a food processor. Work in the wholemeal and barley flours and process thoroughly. Return the starter to the bowl, cover with clear film (plastic wrap) and leave in a warm place for 36 hours.

3 To make the dough, put the yeast and water in a small bowl and cream together. Return the sourdough starter to the food processor, pour in the yeast mixture and process to combine well. Gradually add the wholemeal flour, with the salt, and work the whole dough until it becomes smooth and elastic. Transfer the dough to a lightly oiled bowl, cover with clear film and leave, in a warm place, for 1½–2 hours until nearly doubled in size.

4 Return the dough to the food processor and use the pulse button to work it to a smooth dough. Dust a baking sheet with cornmeal, and shape the dough on it to a plump round. Sprinkle with a little cornmeal. Cover with a large upturned bowl. Leave to rise, in a warm place, for about 1 hour, or until nearly doubled in size.

5 Preheat the oven to 220°C/425°F/Gas 7 and place a roasting pan in the bottom of the oven. Pour 300ml/½ pint/1¼ cups cold water into the roasting pan. Lift the bowl off the risen loaf and put the baking sheet in the oven. Bake the bread for 10 minutes. Remove the pan of water, reduce the oven temperature to 190°C/375°F/Gas 5 and bake for about 20 minutes. Cool on a wire rack.

Nutritional information per loaf: Energy 2265kcal/9588kJ; Protein 81.5g; Carbohydrate 463.5g, of which sugars 10.8g; Fat 17.3g, of which saturates 1.4g; Cholesterol 0mg; Calcium 214mg; Fibre 55.5g; Sodium 17mg.

The Spanish kitchen

This section looks at the various regions of Spain and their influence on the country's cuisine as well as how traditional eating habits have inspired a wide range of dishes. There is also a guide to the different ingredients used in Spanish cooking, and there are many hints on preparation and cooking techniques.

The regions of Spain

The Spanish regions are divided by many mountain ranges. This separates them geographically, but has also led to cultural differences. The climate, too, varies greatly, both across the regions and between seasons. As a result, there are many distinctive local food traditions.

THE SOUTH

Typical images of Spain are of the south: blinding sunshine and a cool arch into a Moorish patio where a guitarist is quietly practising; white walls, covered with pots of bright geraniums; horses parading and girls in polka-dot flounced skirts.

Andalusia This region encompasses the whole of the south coast, looking east on the Mediterranean from Almeria province, south to Africa from Málaga and out on to the Atlantic beyond Gibraltar. Andalusia's greatest foods are green olives and the dried hams of the *sierras* – hence the name *jamón serrano*. A wide variety of shellfish are found in the warm Mediterranean, and from the Atlantic come big fish such as sharks and tuna. In this corner of the province are the sherry *bodegas*, where oak barrels, stacked in dark tiers, mature the precious liquid. Andalusia is said to be the "zone of frying"; but in the villages, old-fashioned stews of beans

ABOVE: *Sun and shade, blinding white walls and pots filled with geraniums are typical of Andalusia's many villages.*

or chickpeas are just as common. *Gazpacho*, a chilled tomato and cucumber soup, is wonderfully refreshing in the midday heat.

Murcia Along the coast to the east lies Murcia, another Moorish province. This is another market garden area, with the *Huerta de Murcia* growing seas of bright green parsley and broad (fava) beans so tender they are cooked in the pod. Stuffed (bell) peppers, tomato salad with cumin and an *escabeche* of aubergines (eggplants) with vinegar are popular. But the region is famous for lemons and pickled capers, and for Calasparra rice, Spain's best and ideal for paella.

CENTRAL SPAIN

At 700m/2,300ft, the *Meseta* is the high heart of Spain and comprises nearly half the country. This is *Castilla* (of the castles), a great plain with

Madrid in the middle, which divides into two rather different halves.

Northern Castile and León *Tierra de pan y vino* (land of bread and wine) is one description of the Duero valley. Bread has mystical significance in the plains of Old Castille, where *hogazas*, big close-grained loaves, are made.

Legumes are daily fare, well-flavoured with garlic. Chickpeas and lentils grow here, and white *alubias* that are used to make bean stews with oxtail or pigs' ears and sausage. The northern fringe, El Bierzo, is very wild, but known for *empanada de batallón*, a pie made with chicken, rabbit, frogs, chorizos and peppers. The old kingdom of León is deeply influenced by the French pilgrim route passing through it, which shows in foodstuffs such as sausages. Best known are Burgos's *morcilla*, a black pudding (blood sausage) with rice, and Cantimpalo's *chorizo*, Madrid's choice for their traditional *cocido*.

Madrid The city's dish is *cocido*, but *callos* (tripe) is so popular that it has moved from the home to become bar fare. Madrid's many restaurants introduced short-order cooking to Spain – *madrileño* is used to indicate quicker dishes. The city is spoiled for fish and delicatessens. In May, the festival of San Isidro is celebrated with mixed salads and puff pastries.

New Castile and La Mancha A hot and dry region, La Mancha's great plains are covered with low vines, with odd corners of saffron planted by the Moors. The intense heat of the summer fuels a preference for strong, robust flavours.

ABOVE: *Water was important to the Moors in Andalusia and the fountains of the Genaralife in Granada irrigate one of their greatest gardens.*

Sopa de ajo (garlic and bread soup) and dishes with cumin are typical of this region.

The food is simple yet delicious – tomato salads, *el asadilla* (baked sweet red peppers) and marinated vegetables such as aubergines (eggplants) pickled in Almalgro in the Moorish fashion. Paprika, which spices red sausages, is made from *choricero* chillies, here and in the neighbouring La Vera valley. Best-known of all, however, is *tortilla* – the thick, solid potato and onion omelette.

Extremadura This region borders Portugal to the west, and is an important area for wildlife. Extremadura is poor and there is a good deal of hunting for free food: birds, rabbits, frogs, freshwater fish and summer truffles. Montanchez and Guijelo are famous for the superb *pata negra* (black foot) hams. The black pigs run wild under the oaks, fattening up on acorns. The locals are great consumers of pork. Everything from the pig that can be is made into sausages, and the rest is either pickled, stewed or minced in some manner. *Migas* (fried breadcrumbs) are served with fry-ups, or combined with bacon and chillies.

THE NORTH COAST

Isolated from the rest of Spain, the wet north has a rugged coast and a Celtic tradition that links it closely to its northern neighbours.

Galicia A wet region, Galicia grows produce for the Madrid markets, including *padrón* peppers, watercress and kiwi fruit. The favourites at home are a special white potato (*cachelo*), turnips and, more particularly, *grelos* – the turnip leaves just coming into bud. The poorer south is covered with chestnut trees, whose nuts were long a basic food but which are now eaten at festivals. Three-quarters of the land provides pasture for dairy cows, whose milk is used to make Galician cheeses such as *tetilla*. Here you will also find the blond breed *rubio*

BELOW: *The fairytale* Alcázar *(fortress) of Segovia is one of the many medieval castles throughout central Spain – giving the region its name, Castile.*

gallego, which supplies much of the country's best meat. Santiago de Compostela cathedral is a place of world pilgrimages. The pilgrims' badge is a scallop shell, because the shell is the symbol of St James of Santiago.

Asturias and Cantabria The range of mountains that run east to west along the north coast stretch 500km/300 miles. Oak and beech woods support spectacular wild life – bears, wolves and wild cats, as well as deer, boar and capercaillie.

This is "green Spain", with some 250 varieties of apple, and where cider-drinking is popular. High up, dairy pastures provide the milk for half of Spain's cheeses. Cantabria, the corridor west from the Basque country, is a coast of small bays and fishing harbours. Sardines are found in abundance and the hake is cooked in cider with mussels and brandy. Squid are breaded and fried.

ALONG THE PYRENEES

Three different provinces border France – the successful Basque country, smaller Navarra and large, poor Aragon.

The Basque country Snuggled into the Pyrenées close to France, el País Vasco has many Michelin-starred restaurants. Long recognized as Spain's finest cooks, the Basques do things the French way, using butter and cream, and take their food seriously. Eating is very social, with an eatery per every 1,000 people. The Basques adopted the *pincho* (a *tapa* on a stick) and are sophisticated tapas crawlers. The Basques also have a long connection with the sea. Cod is mainly fished off the coast of Iceland, to be sold, salted, in *bacalao* shops. Salt fish goes into *zurraputuna*, a soup

with bread and chilli, and *porrusaldo*, soup with leeks, which is eaten mid-morning as the workmen's breakfast.

Navarra This tiny region is isolated, with one highway, the great Valley of Roncesvalles, passed through for hundreds of years by millions of pilgrims on their way to Santiago de Compostela. These travellers ate *bacalao al arriero*, now often a cream of salt cod and garlic, and a hunk of *chistorra* sausage. Mountain dishes include mushrooms with herbs, roast quail in fig leaves and brown trout. Lamb is fried in *cochifrito* or stewed with red (bell) peppers as *chilindrón*.

BELOW: *Vineyards below the castle ruins and church of San Vicente de la Sonsierra, produce excellent wine.*

ABOVE: *Bright yellow sunflowers are grown for their seeds, which are often served as a* tapa, *or crushed to make margarine or cooking oil.*

ABOVE: *Los Cristianos in Tenerife is popular with tourists and and is famed for its excellent tapas bars and restaurants. It still has its own small fishing fleet.*

Aragón This region has a low population density, and therefore large, almost deserted spaces. In the north, the valleys and plains are full of towns but in the south lies Teruel which is almost inaccessible and astoundingly beautiful. Aragón also boasts soaring mountains, with many chamois and boar. Game is a speciality, especially the birds that skim over the mountains. Pigeons are served in *salmorejo* (garlic and vinegar sauce) and partridges with chocolate. The hams of Teruel, one of the three best in the country, are eaten as *magras con tomate* (served in tomato sauce).

THE EAST COAST AND THE ISLANDS

As with the other regions of Spain, the east coast and the islands that lie off the mainland have their own specific culture, flavour and traditions.

Catalonia The French discovered the excellent fish on the Costa Brava, and named it the Wild Coast. Ever since then people visited Catalonia to eat *zarzuela*, a seafood stew, and *susquet*, which includes tomato and potatoes.

Catalan cooking is eclectic. *Aioli* was invented here and was first recorded in 100AD, and saffron and the tradition of combining meat with fruit go back to the Roman times.

Almonds, onions, and aubergines (eggplants) remain popular, while the provincial dish is the chickpea *escudella* with pork dumpling, served in two courses. Quality shows in simple foods such as *pa amb tomàquet* (bread rubbed with garlic, oiled and rubbed with ripe tomatoes.

The Levante The east coast includes Alicante and Valencia and a good many of Spain's sunshine beaches.

Paella was invented here by picnicking men, and it is still customary to have a *tío* (uncle) in charge. Lake Albufera has eels, eaten with pepper (*alli-pebre*). Rice dishes often include runner (green) beans, or *garrafones* (huge flat dried white beans). These are described as "paving stones across rice" in the dish *arros empedrat*. A priest had the idea of planting oranges commercially here in the 1780s. Now they grow year-round along with lemons, dates and muscat grapes. Horchata, a milky drink made from *chufas* (tiger nuts), is a local speciality. It is also a region of festival cakes and Christmas *turrón* (nougat).

The Balearic Islands Mallorca, Menorca and Ibiza are islands with good lobsters and fish, and gulleys full of herbs. The British fleet, which was stationed in Menorca for 150 years, left gin, clover and dairy cows that now provide the milk for the cheese *mahón*. The French discovered *mahonesa* (mayonnaise) here in the 1750s and instantly adopted it. Food tends to be solid, as in the layered-vegetable *tumbet*, along with rich soups, and snails from the earthenware *greixonera*.

Pigs take centre stage, the high point being the exquisite, spreadable, bright orange *sobrasada* sausage.

The Canary Islands *Las Canarias* specialize in local fish, which are beautiful in their varying colours, such as the yellow-purple *vieja*, and cooked simply. They are served with unusual wrinkled potatoes (*papas arrugadas*), which are cooked in sea water and served unpeeled. With them comes *mojo*, a green sauce of blended garlic, coriander (cilantro) and vinegar. A climate of eternal spring produces a wealth of vegetables, including corn.

The social context

The Spanish are a gregarious people and much of their social life revolves around food. Many people breakfast in a bar before going to work or go out mid-morning, and lunch is typically a big affair. However, social eating continues long into the evening.

Spanish breakfasts can involve *café con leche*, *zumo* (juice) and *tostadas* (toast) or, if they are lucky, a sophisticated roll such as an *ensaimada* or *sobao*. For anyone in no hurry, there is always hot chocolate served with *churros* – long strips of deep fried batter for dunking in the thick chocolate drink.

Lunch is a big affair, typically starting at around two o'clock but later on feast days. The old pattern, in middle-class households, was to eat meat at lunch, then fish at night, with vegetables as a first course. Now it is one or the other. Children have a *merienda* (drink and snack) at about five o'clock. Women often meet friends for a *merienda* after work. The whole family gets together for the *paseo* – a seven o'clock promenade. Men might go for an *aperativo*. Supper is late, and is a light meal, often vegetable-based.

RIGHT: *Cafés provide drinks throughout the day, offering a place to pause and relax or to meet friends and family.*

Large cities never seem to sleep. Dinner bookings are made for ten o'clock at night, and in Madrid there is a rush hour at three in the morning as everyone goes home to sleep before starting work at eight that morning. And the famous siesta? The lunch hour, for office workers, is two hours long and is mainly spent talking.

MENUS

Salad is universal as a first course during the hot summer months. Placed in the centre of the table, everyone uses their own fork to eat from it. A restaurant will offer ham or several cold meats, egg dishes, shellfish and soups. The latter are often heavy, and would be regarded as stews elsewhere. Rice and pasta are listed separately, but are a first course in Spain. Then there is a fish or meat course, perhaps offered *a la brasa* or from the *barbacoa* (cooked over charcoal). Restaurants offer desserts, but at home these are usually reserved for saints' days and fiestas.

EATING AT HOME

The Spanish tradition is for slow-cooking, which can really go on all day. The *puchero*, a pot of mixed pulses and meats or sausage, was made most days and left on the stove, wafting rich aromas around the house. At one time, mothers were kept busy in the kitchen but life is different now, and many women work. The delicatessen round the corner stays open until late and supermarkets, with their ready meals, are open all hours.

THE GREAT OUTDOORS

Eating outdoors is part of the Spanish psyche and most houses have balconies and patios, and perhaps a little outdoor summerhouse called a *comedor* (eating place) because it is often too hot to sit out in the sun. Built-in charcoal barbecues grace many gardens.

The Spanish are great picnickers. On casual occasions, family groups may go for a happy day out in the *campo* (fields), or for a harvest picnic. For more formal gatherings such as pilgrimages and fairs, makeshift booths or houses (*casetas*) are put up for entertainment. They offer dining, dance floors and kitchens with gas tripods over which paella is cooked. As many as 2,000 people may be accommodated for the night at unpublicized local events, in tents that are put up and taken down in a single weekend.

RIGHT: *Outdoor cooking is a big part of Spanish life and paella is often cooked for large numbers on festival days.*

EATING OUT

Families eat out together at weekends, with all the generations present. This is one of the reasons why restaurants are so numerous and prices remain so affordable. Hospitality is offered in restaurants rather than at home and many eating establishments advertise catering for large numbers. Jokingly called a *palacio de boda* (wedding palace), big parties celebrate not just weddings but First Communions and golden weddings. Spectacularly tiered cakes may appear at any of the celebrations. These large parties are paid for by the guests, who come with large cash rolls: the bill is paid, then the rest forms the bridal gift.

LOCAL CUISINE

Today freezers and imports may have improved choice somewhat, but essentially Spanish cooking is regional, devoted to locally produced quality ingredients. There is a big emphasis on home cooking and menus that feature local dishes.

Tapas

Tapas are Spain's greatest food invention. "Eat when you drink, drink when you eat" is the philosophy. Tapas are not meant to be a meal (although a ración is a substantial portion). One tapa per person and a different one with each drink is the idea, then everyone enjoys sharing.

The idea comes from Andalusia. It started, so they say, with a piece of bread, soon topped with ham or cheese, balanced over a glass, to keep out the flies – the word *tapa* means a cover. Tapas were once free snacks included in the price of the drink. Now this is a way of life in the south. In dim caverns, where the sherry barrels are stacked high, men revolve the wine in their *copitas*, gently sipping, then select a new wine from a different cask. To compare and contrast is part of the tapas ritual. An old man may sit by the door, with a bucket of *conchas finas*, opening clams slowly and to order. It is a relaxed lifestyle. Tapas bars or *tascas* abound in Spain and you never have to look too far to find one. In Catalonia, there are also busy bars called *champánerías*, where it is customary to sample a glass of the local cava with your tapa.

SOCIAL AMBIENCE

Tapas bars were once the sole preserve of men. Now they are popular with women, too, but they

RIGHT: *A busy traditional bar in Madrid serving tapas and drinks to lunchtime customers.*

BELOW: *This smart tapas bar in Bilbao, decorated with ornate gilt, entices a sophisticated and loyal clientele.*

are still a great place to discuss sport, particularly bullfighting. In this macho atmosphere old foods survive, for example squares of blood (set with vinegar) "to give men strength at night". Tapas also fuel Spain's many fiestas. After all, how could one follow an all-night procession without a bite to eat first? A café terrace is also an ideal place from which to watch.

People may go to tapas bars for the company, but they stay for the food. A range of flavours is offered in tiny portions, from the sophisticated and exotic to the bland and soothing. Tapas are laid out on the counter, like jewels in a shop window: yolk-yellow *tortilla*, kidneys in sherry, red-hot potatoes, and stuffed baby squid.

CLASSIC TAPAS

Tapas dishes revolve around shellfish. In the southern triangle of sherry towns – between Jerez de la Frontera, El Puerto de Santa Maria and Sanlúcar de Barrameda – you may eat amazing shellfish, including squid eggs, whelks (*cañadillas*) and fritters of minute shrimps. The south is also famous for fried fish, *cazón* (a type of shark) marinated in saffron, and *frita malagueña* (mixed battered seafood).

Charcuterie is an important part of the tradition. Hams hang over every bar, with little upturned paper umbrellas underneath to catch dissolving fat: the incomparable scarlet *jamón serrano*.

CITY SPECIALITIES

Each city or region has its own type of tapas. Madrid favours tripe, *boquerones en vinagre* (fresh anchovy fillets cured in vinegar) and shellfish. The old tradition was to throw prawn and shrimp heads on the floor of the bar to show how popular the establishment was.

In Barcelona, designer bars are all the rage and people go there to see and be seen.

Basque bars in cities reflect a much more bourgeois clientele. The phrase *ir de pinchos* means to go for a tapas crawl, which can be a popular way to spend an evening, touring with friends and eating along the way.

In the north, fried tapas often evoke nostalgia, with bechamel-based *croquetas* (croquettes), and *gambas en gabardinas* (prawns/shrimp in batter).

Bars are the place to find local food specialities such as spider crab in San Sebastián, and elvers and hake throats in Bilbao. The morsels can often be very elaborate – high cuisine presented in miniature.

Tapas bars are also a wonderful way to sample some of Spain's best dishes such as *rabo de toro* (bull's tail) and the delicious *escabeche de perdiz* (vinegared partridge).

The story of the olive

Olive trees are one of the oldest Mediterranean crops. The practice of growing olives is thought to have been spread throughout Spain by the Phoenicians before 1000BC. Spain is now the largest producer and exporter of olive oil, most of it from the south.

GROWING OLIVES

The Mediterranean basin is defined by where olives grow. Three-quarters of olive oil comes from southern Spain, but olives also grow to the west as far

ABOVE: *Unfiltered single-olive oils such as this one are new in Spain.*

north as Madrid and to the Pyrenees at Huesca in the east, with a corridor through La Mancha to Valencia.

Olive trees grow on flat or hilly land, but need winter cold as well as warmth to flourish. They blossom in May in an explosion of white flowers. Half of Spain's olives are the *picual* variety, which turn black on the trees before being picked at the end of November. About 4–5kg/8³⁄₄–11lb are needed to make a litre of oil.

In Catalonia, oil-making dates back to Roman times, when Spanish oil was a luxury product. The region's favourite tree, the *arbequina*, produces large amounts of small olives that never turn black, even when fully ripe. The oil is smooth and low in astringency. Catalonia has three *Denominación de Origen* (D.O.) areas: Borjas Blancas in Lérida, Siurana west of Tarragona, and Las Garrigues in the southern part of Lérida.

Andalusia's oil tradition dates back to the Moors. The oil is very fruity, with high astringency. The D.O. areas are Córdoba and Jaén: Baena and Priego de Córdoba in the former, and the Sierra de Segura

and Sierra Magina in the latter. The Montes de Toledo, Murcia and Aragón also have D.O. areas.

OLIVE OIL

The benefits of the Mediterranean diet are owed, in part, to olive oil. The oil is rich in oleic acid, which can help to reduce levels of bad cholesterol and raise levels of good cholesterol. It contains vitamin E, a natural oxidant that helps bone formation in the young and old. It also helps reduce blood pressure and may even be an aphrodisiac for women, for it is high in the female hormone oestrogen.

However, it is for its kitchen virtues that the olive has been cultivated. A simple dressing of virgin oil brings out the flavour of food, cold or hot. Olive oil is also good for frying, as its subtle bitterness counters the rich effect of frying.

The high acidity of Spanish oil makes it ideal for making sauces and emulsions such as dressing and mayonnaise, which was first made in Spain. Once exposed to air, oil should be used within three months, though some top-quality oils may keep well for up to a year.

LEFT: *An unfiltered (opalino) extra virgin green olive oil.*

OLIVE OIL SAUCES

Aliñada Virgin oil is often used as a dressing for cooked food. The name literally means embellished.

Ajada This is north coast food. Fish is fried in the oil, then vinegar and paprika are added to make a sauce.

Aioli Garlic and oil are blended to make a thick, white emulsion, which is served with vegetables. The Catalan *aioli amb ous* is aioli with egg yolk, which is served with fish and rice.

Mahonesa Spanish "mayonnaise" takes its name from Mahón in Menorca. It is a rich emulsion of egg yolk and oil and is more subtle than aioli, from which it is probably derived. It is also the perfect partner for shellfish.

Pil pil Like aioli, this is an emulsified sauce. It combines the gelatine in fish skin with oil. The fish is cooked in the oil, and the oil is then swirled in the hot casserole dish until it thickens.

Negras perlas

Pimiento-stuffed olives

TABLE OLIVES

Spain is the world's chief olive producer, with half the crop being exported. The vast majority of these olives grow on unirrigated land within range of Seville. Spanish cured olives are mainly picked when they are bright green and unripe. At this point, they are low in oil, being made up of only acid and sugars. In this state, the olives will keep their colour as well as their grassy tang for several months after brining. Left on the tree they turn a mottled purple, and finally black, with a softer, fuller flavour. The *muerta* (dead) just drop from the tree, black and wrinkled.

To remove their bitterness, green olives are washed in several changes of water and then stored for a few days in brine (known as the Seville way) with flavourings, to make *aceitunas aliñadas* (seasoned olives). In Andalusia, garlic, oregano and herbs are used while, in the Balearics, wild fennel and lemon leaves are chosen. Pitted olives stuffed with little pieces of cooked pimiento, slivers of almond, anchovy or roasted garlic are also sold, and popularly exported.

Manzanillas

Types of olive

There are over 50 different varieties of olive grown in Spain, with over half of them grown in Andalusia, and each type of olive possesses its own individual appearance and special character.

Arbequina comes from the village of La Arbeca in Lérida. It is very small, greenish-brown and has a high oil content and pleasant bitter-to-aromatic flavour. It is *the* Catalan appetizer.

Cornezuelo is horn-shaped, green and with a white tip. It has a strong flavour with a hint of bitterness.

Cuquillo is round, small, and blue-black. It is often prepared with chopped onion and hot spices, and is good as a partner to beer.

Gordal or reina (queen) are trade names for the largest, dark green, fleshy olive, often called *sevilles* in Spain.

Hojiblanco is slightly rectangular in shape. One of the main types of olives, it is more fibrous and less tasty than other varieties.

Manzanilla is apple- or pear-shaped, the best-known and most popular olive. It is often cured in brine and has a smoky flavour. It is suitable for stuffing with pimiento or garlic.

Pelotín from Andalusia, is small, round and green.

Negra is black, spiced or dried and pickled, and is the perfect accompaniment to red wine. Large negras are called *negras perlas* and are fruity with a mild flavour.

Cheese

Spain produces about 200 varieties of cheese (queso), most of them in farmhouse dairies and with limited distribution. A considerable number are exported, with the hard cheeses being the most successful and Manchego *perhaps the most well known.*

Cheeses in Spain are shaped according to the local traditions. Muslin (cheesecloth) is used to shape the Galician *tetilla* and also *Mahón*, producing very different results. *Camerano* is a ball-shaped cheese, moulded in a basket. Sycamore or maple leaves are pressed on to the wet rind of northern blue cheeses. Esparto grass hoops give Manchego cheese a welt, which becomes broader on the rind of the *Ronda*.

Although goat's, cow's and ewe's milk all produce distinct cheeses with their own unique character, some generic cheeses are made with milk blends. The semi-hard *Aragón*

is made with ewe's and goat's milk, as is *Gamonedo*. Some cheese is smoked – most notably the versions of *San Simón*, *Gamonedo* and *Idiazábal*. *Quesucos* (part of the Liébana D.O.) is a mild, smoked, mixed-milk cheese from Santander, pale yellow inside, with "eyes".

Hard cheeses are often served as a tapas dish, while soft ones are served with honey and nuts as a dessert. There is little in the way of cheese cooking – only fried hard-cheese cubes, and *flamenquines* (ham and cheese rolls that are breadcrumbed and deep-fried).

FRESH AND SOFT CHEESES

Fresh curd cheese (*requesón*) is much liked and made all over Spain. Ewe's milk is normally used to make matured cheese, but there are some soft ones, which include the white *Anso*, from the valley of Huesca; and the mild *Cervera* and *Puzol*, both from Valencia. Two are widely available and typical: *Queso de Burgos* is rindless, often with mould markings, and soft. It is made from scalded curd, which is moulded then salted in

brine for 24 hours. *Villalón* or *pata de mulo*, from the Valladolid region, is an elongated cylinder.

GOAT'S MILK CHEESES

In the south, cheeses are chiefly made with goat's milk. Often pressed, their flavour is distinct and clean. They are not pungent like many of the French varieties of goat's milk cheese, and they have a light, crumbly texture. Unaged goat's milk cheeses include *Alicante*, *Camerano* from the Rioja area, and the slightly aromatic *Málaga*, with its buff rind, lightly pressed into an esparto grass mould.

Southern goat's cheeses include *Cádiz*, which is medium-pressed, full of holes and with a rind marked with esparto, and *Añejo de cabra* from the *Sierra de Huelva*, whose ripened paste is dark orange, with a rough rind. The Canary Islands make only goat's cheese, the best being *Majorero*, which is matured for two months. In the east, *Garroxta* is made all over Catalonia. In central Spain, *Ibores* from Extremadura, is made from retinto goat's milk. It is aromatic, slightly sour, with a soft oiled rind coated with paprika. *Soría* has a firm white skin and is lightly salted. *Cabra de Tiétar*, from Ávila, is lightly pressed and briefly matured. *Valdeteja*, from León, has a sharp, goaty smell. It has some holes and a crusty rind.

LEFT: *Menorcan Mahón is made using cow's milk. Its bright orange rind is produced by rubbing the rind with butter, paprika and oil.*

COW'S MILK CHEESES

In the north, cheeses are made with cow's milk. They are generally eaten quite young and are creamy and soft.

Tetilla, from Pontevedra in Galicia, is white inside, moulded with a cloth and sometimes has a golden rind. Its name literally means teat or nipple, reflecting the shape of the cheese. *Cebrero* (*Piedrafita*), from the mountains of Lugo, is tangy and white inside. The mild, yellow *Gallego* (*Ulloa*) is a slightly flattened ball. *León* is a yellow drum, with a close texture

All about Manchego

Spain's premier cheese is made from the milk of Manchega ewes from the centre of the country. It is a semi-firm cheese with a nutty flavour. It is made in 3kg/6^1/$_2$lb drums, or occasionally smaller. Sometimes pasteurized, the curds are heated and pressed into esparto grass moulds, which pattern the outside of the cheese. Golden inside, Mature (sharp) cheeses are similar to Parmesan.

ABOVE: *Manchego is sold as semi-curado (under 13 weeks), curado (up to six months), viejo (over six months), and also packed in oil.*

and rough yellow rind. The dry *Afuega el pitu*, from Asturias, is shaped in a small cone. *Pasiego prensado*, which is made south-west of Santander, is white and creamy with small holes. *San Simón*, from the Lugo province in Galicia, is oiled on the outside then smoked, but remains creamy inside.

Extremadura produces two soft-rind, creamy cheeses that are unusual for Spain. *La Serena* D.O., made in Cáceres, and *Torta de Casar* are spring cheeses – the latter set with cardoon, which makes it pleasantly bitter. It is usually spooned out of its pink rind.

In the Balearics, *Mahón* D.O., from Menorca, owes its existence to the British, who brought Friesian cows to the island, where the salty grazing affects the cheese's taste. It is hand-pressed into rectangles.

BLUE CHEESES

Cabrales D.O. is a real gourmet cheese made from cow's milk (or sometimes a blend) in 25 x 20cm/10 x 8in drums. A worthy competitor to Roquefort, the paste is off-white with blue veins, and it is slightly stronger and more acidic than the French cheese. It is moulded and dry-salted, then matured for about six months in natural limestone caves in the Asturias and finally wrapped in plane tree leaves. Related cheeses are *Picón* (part of the Liébana D.O.) and *Tresviso*. *Gamonedo*, another Asturian blue made from blended milk, which is unusual both for being smoked for 10 to 12 days before maturing, and for its wrapping of fern leaves. The flesh is blue-veined with oval eyes.

ABOVE: *Idiazábal D.O. (top) has been made for centuries by shepherds in the Urbia and Alara mountains. San Simón (bottom) is a semi-soft cow's milk cheese from Galicia.*

EWE'S MILK CHEESES

In central-north Spain, Castile and León produce most of the ewe's milk. This is the home of hard, pressed cheeses with dark rinds. Made in big drums, they are well-matured, strong, dense and grainy.

Roncal was Spain's first D.O. cheese. The ivory paste has tiny holes. *Idiazábal* D.O., from the Basque Provinces, is a classic, holey, often smoked cheese. *Zamorano* D.O., from western Castile, is unpasteurized, made from the best milk in Spain.

Other firm cheeses include *Grazalema* from Cadiz, *Orduña* from Navarra, the *Oropesa* from Toledo and Basque *Gorbea*. *Pedroches* from Córdoba is piquant and salty, which is enhanced by storing it in oil.

Vegetables

The Spanish really appreciate fresh vegetables. In spring, fresh peas, the first asparagus and shoots of young crops such as garlic are gathered and served in egg dishes and menestras (vegetable stews). New small artichokes (alcachofas) are grilled on the first barbecues of summer.

FRESH VEGETABLES

Growing delicate green asparagus (*espárragos*) is a big industry in the south, in the valleys around Granada, while white asparagus are grown in the valley of the Ebro, in Navarre, and canned for sale all over Europe. Other excellent food crops grow there too, including *cogollos* (Little Gem, or Bibb, lettuces).

Spinach was introduced by the Moors and their *espinacas a la catalana*, with pine nuts and raisins, is still made today. In the south, spinach is replaced by chard (*acelga*) with similar but coarser leaves. The pearly stalks can be battered and fried.

Another popular vegetable of the Islamic lands is *berenjena*, the

aubergine or eggplant (*albergenies* in Catalan). *Almodrote* combines aubergine with garlic, cumin, pine nuts and cheese; *alboronia* is similar to ratatouille, but with no tomatoes.

ONIONS AND GARLIC

The Moors loved onions, especially raw, which is one reason why the Spanish onion, also called the Bermuda onion, is so big and mild. *Sofrito* is the combination of onion and garlic fried together to form the base of numerous sauces. *Cebollones* (*calçots* in Catalan) are oversized spring onions (scallions), with the mild flavour of shallots. Young garlic shoots, plucked when green, are similar and these *ajetes* have a spring cuisine of their own, usually cooked with eggs and seafood. Leeks are popular with the Basques and are used in soups such as *purrusalda*.

Garlic is as old as the Pyramids and is fundamental to Spanish cooking, although it does not dominate it. Many sauces contain this pungent vegetable. *Ajo-pollo*, which means "the sort of sauce used for chicken", combines crushed garlic with ground almonds and breadcrumbs. Valencian *alli-pebre* is a mixture of garlic and paprika, and *aioli* is simply a mixture of garlic and oil – the names say it all.

LEFT: *Leafy green spinach was first introduced to Spain by the Moors and has been popular ever since, particularly in many Catalan dishes.*

ABOVE: *Fresh young turnips and their leafy green tops are Galicia's pride.*

DRIED BEANS, LENTILS AND PEAS

Dried broad (fava) beans are not used as widely as they were in years past, but they are still used in a few dishes today, such as *micherones* (stewed with garlic). Dried peas and lentils (*lentejas*) are still weekly fare, partnered with chorizo, particularly north of Madrid. Chickpeas (*garbanzos*) are the potatoes of Spain. Although they take time to prepare, they keep their shape well.

RIGHT: *Large Spanish onions are sweet and mild enough to eat raw.*

WILD MUSHROOMS

The Spanish in general are not great mushrooms pickers except for the Basques and Catalans. About 50 kinds are gathered during the year. They are cooked simply, with garlic or eggs, and are used in game casseroles.

TOMATOES

Today, tomatoes are a great success story in Spain. Three or even four crops a year are produced in the *invernadores* (plastic tunnels) of Almería. The name *tomate* comes from the Aztec *tomatl*, meaning something plump. The tomato was not an instant success when it was introduced to Spain and was still a novelty as late as the 1820s.

FRESH PEPPERS

Morrones (bell) peppers, are often two-fist size, fleshy with tough skin, green or the sweeter red. When soft and baked, red pepper has become an ingredient in its own right, *pimiento*.

The red *piquillo*, grown in Navarra and Rioja, is the gourmet's pepper. It is often stuffed with cod and baked. It is also wonderful canned, after being roasted over beechwood.

Green Galician peppers, *padrón*, are part of a popular joke. They are deep-fried and served as an appetizer, about 20 to a plate. Though normally sweet, one in that number will be fiery hot, and there is no knowing which.

RIGHT: *Sweet peppers go into many dishes. Little* padróns *are a Galician speciality, popular everywhere.*

FAR RIGHT: *In the south, squash is added to gypsy vegetable and bean stews.*

DRIED CHILLIES

Columbus's mission was to look for the spice, black pepper. He discovered spicy red peppers instead. Towards winter, chilli peppers are hung up all over Spain to dry, particularly in Rioja, in red *ristras* (strings).

The general rule for chillies is the larger, the milder. Cooking, especially roasting, makes them sweeter, as the bitterness is in the skin. The flavour of chillies is made more concentrated and robust by drying or toasting. Including vinegar in the recipe gives the same intensified effect.

Choricero This chilli has given its name, colour and piquancy to the red Spanish frying sausage. It can be crumbled into dishes or reconstituted in liquid, then the flesh scraped out. One or two per person go into dishes such as *chilindrón*, (lamb with chilli).

Ñora This is called *romesco* in Catalonia and is a walnut-sized chilli; red and cherry-round. It has very little flesh but the colour and flavour are concentrated, hence its use in salsas, *romescos* of fish, rice and paella.

Guindilla As long as a finger, this is Spain's hot chilli – 3/10 on the Mexican chilli-heat scale – but it is also medium sweet. It adds zip to dishes such as *gambas pil pil* (prawns/shrimp with chilli).

POTATOES AND SQUASH

While potatoes were ignored in northern Europe, they were a huge success in Seville. They found their true home in Galicia, which now grows *cachelos*, a large white tuber of exceptional quality, near the sea, where it absorbs salt from the soil.

Sweet potatoes are *batata* (yellow-fleshed; the US yam) and *boniato* (white-fleshed). They are made into little cakes or served in honey.

The *calabaza* (marrow/large zucchini, summer squash or pumpkin) goes into stewpots like *calabazote*. But *calabacín* (courgette/zucchini) was little known until the 1980s.

Spices, herbs and flavourings

The Spanish cuisine has its own range of spices, herbs, condiments and nuts, all of which contribute to the unique and characteristic taste of Spanish food.

SAFFRON

With its aromatic scent and golden colour, *azafrán* is a quintessentially Moorish spice. For paella and fish and shellfish stews, there is no substitute. For chicken, all *pepitorias* (nut sauces), creams, buns and ices, saffron is king. The purple crocuses from which saffron is obtained flower quite suddenly in mid-October in parched La Mancha, creating purple carpets around the vines. The flowers are plucked by hand, then three orange

stamens are carefully pulled from each flower, toasted over charcoal and then dried to bring out the flavour. A day's work produces only about 50g/2oz saffron.

Mancha selecto is the world's best saffron; it is deep red, with long threads and a high oil content. Spain produces 70 per cent of the world's saffron. Although very expensive, a tiny amount flavours a dish for two to three people.

PAPRIKA

Pimentón is a basic flavouring in Spanish cooking, used like black pepper, and not just sprinkled for decoration. It is used to season soups and stews but is also used as an ingredient in sausages. It is made from a sweet red (bell) pepper with a round body and pointed end. There are three grades of paprika used in Spain: *dulce* (mild), *picante* (which contains a

ABOVE: *Warm, spicy, aromatic cumin is a legacy of the Moors and is widely used in southern cooking.*

little *guindilla* chilli), and *agridulce* (bittersweet). If necessary, you can substitute cayenne pepper for the *picante* grade.

HERBS

Bay leaves (*hojas de laurel*) Partnered with rosemary and thyme, aromatic bay leaves make up Spain's herbal trinity. The leaves are added to stews and thrown on the barbecue. Fresh leaves are battered, fried and sugared to make sweet *paparejotes*. **Coriander** (*cilantro*) Pungent fresh

ABOVE: *Top quality saffron all comes from Spain, grown in La Mancha.*

Other spices

The Moors introduced cumin (*comino*) to Spain and it is widely used with vegetables and skewered meats. Coriander seeds (*cilantro*) also came from North Africa, and are often partnered with cumin and used to flavour skewered meat cooked on the barbecue. Coloured yellow with turmeric, pork cubes are sold ready-spiced in many southern butchers. Other popular spice flavourings include turmeric (*cúrcuma*), cloves (*clavos*), cardamom (*cardamoma*) and – to a lesser extent – ginger (*jengibre*).

The Catalans are generous users of black pepper (*pimienta*), whereas the rest of Spain tends to prefer the flavour of paprika (*pimentón*).

There is no clear division between sweet and savoury spices in Spain. Nutmeg (*nuez moscada*) goes into *morcillas* (black pudding) – along with cumin, cinnamon (*canela*) and aniseed (*matalhuva*) – and is also used to flavour custards.

Aniseed (*anís*) is a key flavour in Spanish food and drink. It is basic to many liqueurs and its seeds are ground and used in many pastries, doughs and sausages.

ABOVE: *Many varieties of thyme grow in the Spanish sierras.*

LEFT: *Pine nuts have a distinctive taste and are frequently toasted before being added to dishes.*

ABOVE: *Hazelnuts are used to flavour sweet dishes such as desserts, cakes and cookies, as well as savoury sauces.*

coriander leaves are thought of as the Portuguese herb and only used in Extremadura and the Canary Islands, where the herb is crushed to make the green *mojo verde* sauce for fish.

Fennel (*hinojo*) This beautiful herb has a slight flavour of aniseed and grows wild everywhere. It is used to flavour the cooking water for shellfish and its tiny aromatic seeds can be added to home-cured olives.

Lemon verbena (*hierba luisa*) Used to make a delicious fragrant tea, this popular herb can be found growing in many Spanish gardens.

Mint (*menta*) Known as *hierba buena*, the good herb, Moroccan mint is a favourite garden plant. It goes into *morcilla* (black pudding) and is used with offal.

Oregano (*origano*) This is the sausage herb, and also goes into meat stews and marinades. Its essential oil doesn't deteriorate with long cooking, so it is one of the few herbs that can be added early on in cooking.

Parsley (*perejil*, or *julivert* in Catalan) The Spanish grow flat leaf parsley,

which is milder than curly parsley. It is a popular herb and is used lavishly in Murcia near the Mediterranean coast in southern Spain.

Rosemary (*romero*) Snails eat rosemary, so they are used as "rosemary cubes" to flavour rabbit stews and paella. Big old bushes of the wild herb are also used to fuel bread ovens and wood-burning stoves. Rosemary with thyme and chilli are traditionally used to flavour dried bean dishes.

Thyme (*tomillo*) There are several varieties of thyme with small white flowers, which are used for cooking. *Tomillo salsero* (sauce thyme) is picked in April to give to friends at Christmas. The herb is much used to flavour rabbit and, with summer savory (*ajedrea blanca*), to flavour dried bean dishes.

NUTS

Almonds (*almendras*) These are second only to oranges as a major crop. There are two types. The first is the smaller, bitter almond, which is grown only for almond oil and essence (extract), as it is poisonous if eaten raw. The second type is the sweet *Jordan* almond. Of Spanish origin, its name is a corruption of *jardín* meaning garden. Grown in the south-east, they are long, flat and slender, and the best cocktail almonds in the world. *Marcona* almonds are used to make *turrón* (nougat).

Ground almonds are used in place of flour to thicken sauces in Spain. Almonds are also pounded for soups, used in biscuits (cookies) and coated with sugar to make festival *almendras garipinadas* and Catalan *ametlles*.

Hazelnuts (*avellanas*) These nuts grow in mountain regions and were farmed in Tarragona, where they are made into a soup. The Basques use them to thicken stews, and they are added to meringues as far apart as Granada and Asturias.

Pine nuts (*piñones*) These come from the cones of the stone pine, one of the West's ancient fertility symbols. The tiny creamy nuts have a slightly astringent taste and are improved by toasting, which brings out and enhances their subtle flavour. They are good with raisins, used in salads and sauces, or baked in little cakes, such as festival *paneletts* and nut-covered *piñonates*.

Pasta and rice

These two staples are at the heart of both everyday family meals and classic celebration dishes in Spain. Rice is the main ingredient of one of Spain's most famous dishes – incomparable paella.

PASTA

It sounds very strange to say, but noodles and pasta have actually been eaten in Spain for longer than in north Italy. (There is even a recipe for a noodle soup in Catalonia's first printed cook book, by Rupert de Nolan, in 1477.) Pasta then went on to become everyday food in Spain and Italy at around much the same time, in the late 18th century. Durum wheat, used to make pasta, was planted in Catalonia in the 1950s. Today pasta is made in Andalusia and Extremadura.

The Catalan favourite is *fideos*, a thin, short spaghetti (about 5cm/2in long) used in soups or served with sauces and sausage. South of paella country is Gandía (home of the Borgias, the family of Pope Alexander VI) where they have a *fideuá* (noodle) festival every year.

The big pasta dish these days is shellfish with *fideos* instead of rice, which is a great deal easier to make than paella. It was invented in the 1970s and now features along the entire coast from Málaga to the Costa Brava, including one version where the pasta is dry-fried first.

Canelones (cannelloni) were introduced to Spain by the many Italian chefs who came to work in Barcelona in the 19th century. Flat dry squares, known as *obleas* (thin wafers), are now sold for making lasagne or for rolling into *canelones*.

Home-made pasta was originally made by poor shepherds. They added

ABOVE: *Fideos is a thin and short Spanish pasta – about 5cm/2in long.*

simple flour-and-water paste squares (called Manchego wafers) to stews such as *andrajos*.

RICE

Valencia is forever linked with rice. The Moors planted rice there as it was the only crop that could be grown on the hot Mediterranean littoral in summer. Rice is eaten almost daily in the east and south of Spain. It is eaten plain, added to soupy stews, and combined with beans to make stuffings for vegetables. Many *morcillas* (black puddings/blood sausages) contain rice, especially those made in Burgos, Aragón, Rioja and the Levante. *Arroz con leche* (rice pudding) rivals *flan* (baked custard) as Spain's national dessert.

It is the quality and flavour of rice that matters, so flavourings tend to be simple – a pinch of saffron, perhaps with a little bacon and *morcilla*. Alicante *arros amb costra*, a Catalan oven-baked dish, comes with a rice crust concealing the chickpea and sausage stew. *Arros perdiu* (partridge rice) is "trick dish" made for Lent – instead of partridge, it has a

Spanish rice

The two types of short grain rice, *Bomba* and *Calasparra* (see below), grown in Spain are used to make the classic dish paella as well as other rice dishes.

ABOVE: *Although it can be hard to find, Bomba is excellent for making paella.*

ABOVE: *The prized Calasparra rice is sold in numbered cotton bags.*

whole baked garlic bulb in the centre. Valencian restaurants feature a different rice every day, but the popular choice for Sundays is rice with salt cod.

Short grain rice

The short, fat Spanish grain originates from Japanese round rice, rather than the Indian long grain, and it has a slight bite to it more like Italian risotto rice. In fact, Spain became Europe's largest rice producer because it was the first country to try to find a suitable grain for the Mediterranean climate.

A large amount of rice is grown in the Seville area but the best type of rice is *Calasparra*, which grows in Murcia. The grains are exceptionally dehydrated and so they swell dramatically when cooked in stock, absorbing three or four times their volume of liquid.

Paella

The birthplace of paella is the marshland outside the city of Valencia, round Lake Albufera. The area is still a place of ducks and eels. Bamboo groves in water separate lake from lake and little bridges carry small roads from village to village. El Palmar, one of the best-known villages, is surrounded by water.

Paella was invented here some 200 years ago. It is a summer dish, intended for picnics, generally cooked by men in a special wide two-handled pan set over a charcoal fire. Paella pans are around 33–35cm/13–14in in size, but a smaller pan can be used. Originally, paella used ingredients from the surrounding area – rice, garlic and parsley, either eels or snails, plus good quality beans, which could

either be flat green beans that look like runner beans or big flat kidney beans known as *garrafones*. The seasoning was Spain's best – saffron – while the snails added a hint of rosemary. The rice is cooked very slowly, then covered with newspaper for the last 10 minutes, until all liquid has been absorbed. The paella is allowed to crisp slightly underneath before serving.

Saffron-yellow *paella valenciana*, decorated with mussels and strips of red (bell) pepper, prawns (shrimp) and chicken pieces like buried treasure, is eaten in Spain on every festive occasion. In Valencia, however, it is more of a tourist dish. Locals are more likely to opt for just shellfish or chicken; on the south coast, the usual choice is rabbit.

BELOW: *Paella, originally from Valencia, is eaten for celebrations but is also an incredibly popular dish with tourists.*

Fish and shellfish

Spain is second only to Japan in fish consumption, with over 500g/1lb eaten per head per week. The two coasts of Spain are very different. The Atlantic breaks on Cape Finisterre, where the best fish in the world are found, while the Mediterranean has an abundance of shellfish.

EVERYDAY FISH

The most popular everyday fish is salt cod (*bacalao*), then *pescadilla* – a small hake which is fried in a ring, with its tail in its mouth – and many small flat fish such as *gallo* (a type of plaice).

Sardines have an honoured place in Spanish cuisine, with festivals in Bilbao and elsewhere dedicated to the fish. They are enjoyed as an outdoor food and the *moraga*, on the Málaga coast, marks the beginning of summer: fish are skewered on to bamboo sticks, like sails on a tall mast, and are cooked beside the fires on the beaches. Mackerel, *caballo* and *melva* (from warm water) are other popular fish.

LUXURY FISH

Sea bass (*lubina*), turbot (*rodaballo*) and monkfish (*rape*, or *pixin* as it is known in Asturias) are cooked in wine and shellfish sauces, or with cider.

Dorada, the gilthead bream is the finest Mediterranean bream. Like the related *urta*, the sea bream lives on a diet of shellfish, which scents the flesh. Sea bream can be grilled *a la plancha* and is most famously cooked with brandy and tomatoes.

Hake (*merluza*), with its delicate flavour is extremely popular and highly prized in Spain. Red mullet (*salmonetes*) is also beloved by everyone in Spain.

Anchovies are one of the best fish for frying and may be presented Málaga-style, fried in a fan pattern.

TUNA, SWORDFISH AND SHARK

Tuna are landed at Vigo, from ships that trawl the world. Tuna steaks are meaty and nutritious, and may be fried, grilled (broiled) or cooked on the barbecue. *Bonito del norte*, white tuna, is cooked in stews with (bell) peppers and potatoes.

Swordfish (*pez espada*) cut into steaks is ideal for grilling. Dogfish (*cazón*) and sharks such as *cailón* (porbeagle/mackerel shark) are excellent marinated and grilled.

Bacalao

Salt cod can be eaten at any time of the day. The fishermen in the north eat it for breakfast as *zurruputuna* (salt cod prepared with garlic, chillies and soaked bread). *Purrusaldo* is a robust soup made with salt cod, leek and potato. *Potaje de cuaresma*, made with salt cod, chickpeas and chard, is eaten during Holy Week. The Cuenca area has a brandade-style dish, a purée of fish, potato and pine nuts.

Salt cod requires a minimum of 24 hours soaking, with 2–3 changes of water. In Andalusia the custom is to toast the fish first, break it up and then soak it. This has produced a range of dishes called *tiznao* that taste faintly of the fire.

BELOW: *Delicately flavoured hake is one of Spain's best-loved fish.*

BELOW: *Brown and rainbow trout flourish in the rivers and lakes of Spain.*

FRESHWATER FISH

Spain has many fast-flowing rivers in its mountainous regions. Trout catches in some Pyrenees rivers run at 1,500 a day. León has about 3,000km/1,800 miles of trout rivers, as well as lakes. Brown trout abound in the rivers of western Asturias. *Rea* (sea trout or salmon trout) run up the Galician *rías* (coastal inlets). Brown trout with *jamón serrano* is a famous combination.

Salmon teem in the rivers of Galicia and swim up into the Picos de Europa. The classic salmon recipe is to salt them for one hour, then fry in pork fat. *Lamprea* (lamprey) follow the salmon, especially in the river Miño, while other fish, such as tench, carp and barbel are very much in evidence in Extremadura in summer.

SHELLFISH

Atlantic currents, sweeping on to Cape Finisterre, bring food to an incredible range of shellfish on Europe's most westerly corner, to the Galician *rías* (coastal inlets) and the Spanish north coast. In these waters shellfish grow at great speed. In the Mediterranean the continental shelf is perfect for shellfish.

Scallops, mussels and clams

Santiago de Compostela is famous for scallops, and the pilgrims have chosen their shell for their badge. Today, scallops are farmed in bays to the west. Scallops may be breadcrumbed and fried, cooked with wine and chilli, or with tomato sauce (St James' style).

The mussel beds of Galicia are famous, and Tarragona in the east is also an important area. The bivalves are grown on ropes secured to platforms. In Galicia, 2.5 million mussels are canned per day, and there are plenty of fresh ones too. They are large enough to be breadcrumbed and fried, although wine and parsley mixture are more usual.

In Spain clams are common fare. They are fished on both coasts, but the northern ones are plumper. There are many varieties; one of the best is the *almeja fina*. Most magnificent is the *concha fina*, which measures 8cm/3in across.

Prawns and shrimp

Saltwater varieties are fished on both coasts. In size order:

Camarones These are the tiniest Spanish shrimps and are caught around Cadiz. They turn white and are made into delicious little fritters.

Quisquilla This term covers all the smaller varieties that are caught off the Spanish coasts.

Gamba These have a good colour and are fished reasonably deep, giving them a good flavour.

Langostino These are the longest Mediterranean prawn, fished from deep water. Sometimes they are called tiger prawns.

Carabinero These prawns grow to 20cm/8in long and are a deep scarlet colour with a violet head.

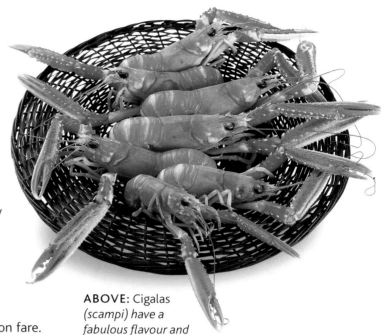

ABOVE: Cigalas *(scampi) have a fabulous flavour and are fished on every coast.*

Lobsters and crabs

Bogavante, the true lobster, is party fare, while *langosta*, the spiny lobster (saltwater crayfish) is eaten to celebrate Spain's national day.

Small shore crabs are served boiled, and picked to pieces at the table. *Buey de mar* (ox of the sea) is the large-clawed crab, but the favourite is the spider crab (*centollo* in Castilian).

Squid, cuttlefish and octopus

Common to both oceans, squid are a popular food. There are many varieties of squid. They are commonly sold cut into rings for stews and should be cooked fast or very slowly, otherwise they will become rubbery.

Cuttlefish, called *jibia* or *sepia*, and *chocos* and *chiperones* if tiny, are similar to squid.

Octopus are popular in the north. They are mainly cooked with paprika, as in *pulpo de feria*, or stewed.

Poultry and game

Poultry cluck around the many farms of Spain and are used in many dishes. Feathered game such as pigeons are very popular and rabbits are commonly eaten.

CHICKEN

More popular now than it used to be, there was a time when chicken was more expensive than beef. The well-known Catalan dish, chicken with lobster, recalls its luxury status.

Gallina is a boiling hen. In *gallina en pepitoria*, it is simmered slowly, then the sauce is thickened with ground nuts. Capons are sold in the Christmas market in Villalba in Galicia. These large birds weigh about 5kg/11lb. Some are fattened on maize (like foie gras ducks) and they are sold in Madrid dressed and stuffed with Roquefort or chestnuts.

Chicken offal (variety meats) is widely used. The gizzards are added to lentil dishes, and accompany the chicken meats in *arroces* (rice dishes). Chicken livers cooked in sherry is a popular tapas dish.

ABOVE: *Huge capons are a favourite at Christmas time.*

ABOVE: *Teal is one of the smallest wild ducks and is highly prized for its fabulous taste and texture.*

Other poultry

Goose and duck are cooked in Catalonia, but are not popular in the rest of Spain. Goose with pears (*oca amb peras*) is the famous dish of the region. The Catalans combine birds and fruit, and the reason is not hard to discover – the birds feed on fruit. Duck is combined with figs in another Catalan classic. Ducks (*pato*) are also reared in Valencia near lake Albufera.

Catalonia and Navarra now breed the mallard, which is a cross between the white duck and the grey barbary, known as *anèc* in Catalan. Teal, a relative of the mallard, is found on lakes and salt flats. Because of the French influence in these regions, foie gras and duck confit are produced. In Galicia, a popular dish combines duck with turnips. However, Spain's most famous recipe comes from Seville. The juice of the Seville orange was added to duck to cut through the fat. Olives do the same job, and there are dishes that combine duck and olives.

The turkey was introduced to Europe via Spain in the 16th century from America. Called *pavo*, after the peacock (*pavo real*), it was cooked like a peacock, stuffed and inserted into a pig's caul. The dark bronze turkey is the bird of choice, weighing in at 3kg/6^1/$_2$–7lb. The best birds come from Aspe, in the Pyrenees.

The guinea fowl (*pintada*) came from Queen Dido's Africa – either directly, or with the Romans. They are now reared in Spain, as are quails (*codornices*).

FEATHERED GAME

There are massive migrations of birds across Spain twice a year, on their way to and from Africa. The 27,000 Spanish shooting clubs try to ensure that two-thirds of the birds pass through their land, for breeding. Small birds have always contributed to the poor family's diet: fieldfare, starling, and even sparrow, can be added to many rice dishes.

Pigeon

Present all year, pigeons (*palomas*) are netted as they fly over the mountains. They are pot-roasted with vinegar, or with raisins in the Val d'Arran, and stewed with peas or mushrooms in Castile. Murcia has a famous pigeon pie, which mimics the highly spiced Moroccan *b'stilla* (a pie made with filo pastry and a filling of shredded pigeon, ground almonds and spices), revealing its distinct Moorish influences. The pie is then baked in the oven until golden and sprinkled with icing (confectioners') sugar and ground cinnamon.

Pheasant

Because it was recorded by the great French chef, Escoffier, *faisan al modo de Alcántara*, pheasant stuffed with duck liver and truffles, became the most famous bird dish in Europe.

Partridge

The partridge in Spain is the red-legged (French) *perdiz* (which is larger than the grey-legged variety). It is far and away the most popular of game birds. Celebrated recipes include partridges in chocolate, Pyrenean mushroom stews, and *perdices en escabeche* (a salad of jellied, vinegared birds).

Quail

In Spain, it is said to rain quails, rather than cats and dogs, because there are so many of these tiny birds (about 10 million). They are trapped in their thousands as they fly south each April. The birds are roasted, barded with bacon and stuffed with their own innards, or casseroled with wine and garlic, or with grapes. A speciality is *codornices con pochas*, quail with freshly shelled haricot (navy) beans, as their seasons coincide.

BELOW: *Tiny quail are one of the most prevalent wild birds found in Spain.*

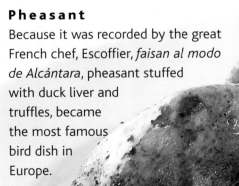

FURRED GAME

Ninety per cent of Spain is mountainous and full of game. The mountain goats are the long-horned ibex (*cabra monte*) and the short-horned chamois (*rebeco* in Catalan). Boars (*jabalí*) are hunted in the rugged north and in the southern mountains.

Hare

In Extremadura, hare (*liebre*) is served at engagement parties, the sauce finished with blood, sherry and brandy. It is also often cooked with chocolate. Sometimes it is cooked in the field, in a pot with charcoal on the lid, and accompanied by beans.

Rabbit

There are rabbits (*conejos*) all across Spain. They are often cooked with snails, which impart the flavour of rosemary, or wild thyme.

Venison

The red *ciervo común* is Europe's largest deer, pre-eminent in the Sierra Morena and the mountains of the south, in the coastal Coto Doñana, and reintroduced into the northern Cantabrian *cordillera*. Venison (*venado*) is cooked in wine, roasted or grilled (broiled) and served with a creamy *Cabrales* sauce.

Pork, ham and sausages

The pig represents Spain's history and religion on the plate. To eat pork and sausages became, after the unification of the country at the end of the fifteenth century, a way of demonstrating nationality as the Muslim Moors and the Jews were forbidden to eat pork.

PORK AND BACON

Almost every family would once have owned a pig. People in the villages would throw rubbish into local gullies and streams, and this was eaaten by foraging pigs. The *matanza* (pig killing), when families gather to make sausages and black puddings (blood

The black wild pig

The native *ibérico* pig is known by its black trotter (*pata negra*). There are actually four dark-skinned breeds, the main two having black or red hair. The pigs are trim and graceful, with long legs. They run wild in small groups, in the sierras of Andalusia and particularly in Extremadura, in the flower pastures called the *dehesa*.

Their numbers are decreasing as their fame rises. Their final food is acorns, which give the meat its full flavour and an old golden tinge. If meat is labelled *bellota*, it means the pig was fed entirely on acorns.

sausage) and celebrate, is the greatest non-religious festival of the year.

Cured meat is eaten more often than fresh, but pork chops and pork loin are Spain's most familiar meat. *Solomillo*, which means fillet of beef in the north, becomes pork in the south; it is delicious *a la trianera* (roasted with sherry). *Magro* is a pork steak that is served with tomato sauce or potatoes.

Other cuts of pork are cured, as well as the ubiquitous ham. In the north, the famous cured meat is *lacón*, a front-leg ham. Among the *salazones* (salted meats), there is coarse-salted belly, and also *panceta* (streaky bacon), which is sometimes marinated before being cured and/or smoked. *Torreznos* are pork slices, fried like bacon and served with eggs.

HAM

Spain produces some of Europe's finest hams, one-third of which are exported. About one-fifth of Spanish pigs are used for hams, so it is not surprising more ham is eaten in Spain than elsewhere in Europe – the Basques alone eat nearly one whole ham each per year.

The mountain-cured *jamón serrano* rules supreme, but lesser hams – *jamón cocido* – are cured for boiling. The front leg of the pig (*paleta*, or *lacón* in Galicia) is also cured. It is a coarser cut but with an even flavour. In the north-west it is used for *caldo gallego*, while *lacón con grelos* (with turnip tops) is the national dish.

ABOVE: *Spanish* panceta *is fresh or cured belly. If it is unavailable, Italian pancetta makes an excellent substitute.*

Jamon serrano

Serrano is the adjective from *sierra* (mountain). It means mountain ham, and indicates that it is raw and dried in cold air. Typically, these hams are long and thin, and almost triangular at the meaty end. Better ones have the trotter (foot) still attached. Thinly sliced *serrano* is eaten for tapas or sandwiched with cheese, but it can also be used to wrap fish. Little batons are added to salads and bean dishes.

SAUSAGES

The pig is virtually a "larder on trotters" and is valued more for what can be made out of it than for fresh meat. It is turned into sausages, frequently home-made, which will last the whole year round. The raw pork is minced (ground), or hand-chopped, mixed with back fat and delicious spices, then stuffed into casings.

Smoked sausages are found across Spain. The dried sausages used in the Asturian *fabada* (pork and bean stew) are smoked and swell with cooking.

Sausages tend to be classed by colour, and this provides some guidance as to how they should be cooked and served. Many dried sausages may be eaten raw, although this is not always the rule.

Black sausages

Morcillas are blood puddings, and are the first to be made from the newly killed pig, straight after slaughter. They are made as links, or as rings in Seville and Ronda in the south. These wonderful sausages are a speciality of the north, the most famous being those of Extremadura and Asturias, which are flavoured with aniseed and cloves, and plumped with either rice or onions. Rice is typically used in some parts of Aragón, and the Burgos *morcilla* also contains pine nuts. *Botifarra* is the black sausage from the east of the country It is made in links, or occasionally in rings.

Red sausages

Paprika is used in sausages across Spain, apart from in Catalonia, the Levante and the Balearics (except for the *sobrasada* from Majorca). Chorizos are named after the *choricero* chilli that gives them both spiciness and colour. There are at least 50 varieties of chorizo, but two main types.

Red chorizos, made in links, contain minced (ground) meat, which is mottled with fat. They may be fried or boiled. The second type is the tapas or cured chorizo. The meat filling is stuffed into a larger gut casing and so is much longer and fatter. These are sliced thinly and eaten with bread, or they are cut into little batons and added to salads.

White sausages

Sausages that are neither black nor red are classified as white sausage, although they are not necessarily white in appearance. The cured varieties are a dark cerise colour inside and are cased in the smaller gut. *Salchichón* comes in rings and strings, and is usually powdered on the outside with ambient bacteria. Some famous examples are made in Vic in Catalonia. *Fuet* is a Catalonian sausage containing white pepper and sugar. It is long and thin so dries fast, and is consequently very chewy.

White *botifarras* (known as *blancas*) are the brothers of the black ones. These fresh sausages are usually grilled (broiled), and are often eaten with beans all along the east coast.

OFFAL

It is said that everything from the pig can be eaten except its squeak, and the pig is the principal source of offal (variety meats) in Spain.

Pigs' heads and tails can be salted. Pickled ears are breaded and fried, as well as being used to make some wonderful delicatessen salads. Trotters and tails may be found in stews and rice dishes. Ham bones are used to flavour beans; as they grow older they become highly prized. Pig's caul is used to baste faggots, and ham fat (*unto*) sold in rolls, is used for frying.

Black and white botifarras

Salchichones

Fuet

Beef, veal, lamb and kid

The varieties of meat available in Spain are far wider than elsewhere. Most people eat some type of meat; there is virtually no vegetarian cooking. Pulse and vegetable dishes are invariably flavoured with sausages and fat.

BEEF AND VEAL

The Spanish have never been great beef eaters. Richard Ford, a century ago, remarked that "bulls are bred for baiting and oxen for the plough, not the spit".

High temperatures elsewhere mean the best beef comes from the north, and Galicia produces about two-thirds of all the beef produced in Spain. However, new breeding programmes, and the modern practice of moving cattle indoors, means more beef is now being produced in Catalonia, Aragón and the cereal plains of Castile. Only the Basques will eat "bloody" meat, and red meat is exported in return for veal cattle.

Hung beef is a northern taste, and vast *chuletones* (chops) are enjoyed in this region. Cattle are slaughtered at between two and five years old to produce *carne de buey* (ox) or *vaca* (cow). This lesser quality beef is stewed, famously with chocolate, or with vegetables as in the Catalan *estofat*. Meatballs are sold in bars and are loved by children, too. Cuts such as salt brisket go into stews; *añojo* means yearling although, in fact, the cattle are slaughtered at between 10 and 18 months. Joints of meat are frequently labelled with their age and diet.

Veal calves are never intensively reared in Spain as they are elsewhere in Europe, and they are often four times the age of Dutch or Italian

ABOVE:
Ox tail, or bull's tail, is a popular choice of meat for stews.

calves when they are slaughtered. Only in the high walled town of Ávila are calves killed very young. Veal escalopes may be braised with vegetables or fried. *Filetitos* are small escalopes fried with lemon juice, and it needs six or seven of them to make up a single portion. Veal is wonderful with artichokes and sherry, and it can also be made into excellent flavoursome stews.

LEFT: *Brisket is a popular addition to stews such as cocido. Cuts from ox or cow are used to make casseroles.*

BELOW: *Veal fillet is usually cut into escalopes. One universal dish is San Jacobo, in which the fillet is topped with serrano ham, then cheese.*

The Moorish oven

Domed ovens built of adobe (roofing bricks), which hold the heat, rather than firebricks, are prized for roasting tiny lambs and piglets particularly in Castile, in places such as Aranda de Duero and Haro. These ovens are part of the restaurant structure, and are about 2m/6ft in diameter inside. They are wood-fired, and cooking only takes place when the glowing charcoal subsides. The burned-out coals are pushed to the side, the dishes are put into the oven using long paddles, then the door is sealed. In the hot south, similar ovens are built outside houses for domestic use.

The fighting bull

A bull is either slaughtered at the age of one, and the meat is minced (ground), or it lives a life of luxury until it comes to the ring at the age of three or four. The meat from these bulls (*toro de lidia*) is sold in specialist shops. The meat is deep black-red and is eaten as steaks in sherry in Jerez, or minced or stewed.

LAMB AND KID

These meats are very expensive, but are still the traditional meat in the grazing regions of central and western Spain, and up into the mountains of Aragón and Murcia. Elsewhere, it is an Easter or wedding treat. Thyme is used to flavour roast lamb. Lamb chops are popular, and tiny legs of lamb provide an exquisite eating experience. Stews can consist of a whole animal, chopped. *Cochifrito* is

ABOVE: *In Spain, legs of lamb may be very small – with one leg per person.*

ABOVE: *Kid is a luxury meat that often replaces lamb in traditional stews.*

flavoured with lemon or vinegar and paprika; *chilindrones*, around Logroño traditionally feature a mild red chilli pepper. *Menestra* are spring stews cooked with young vegetables.

Mutton is used in a few dishes in Aragón and Extremadura, and some

of the classic stews such as *chilindrón* and *caldereta* originally used mutton.

Kid (*cabrito* or *choto*) is usually either roasted on a spit or cooked in stews such as *tumbet* in Valencia or *caldereta extremeña*, which is thickened with the kid's puréed liver.

Spanish stews

Olla puchero Both these words mean cooking pot, the large vessel used to make the daily stew cooked by many families in Spain.

Olla podrida Literally meaning rotten pot, this stew is actually a hotchpotch – a mixed stew of meat and vegetables, simmered until ingredients become soft textured.

Cocido This is shorthand for mixed stew, meaning boiled or simmered.

Cocido madrileño This is the national dish, where several different meats are cooked with chickpeas and vegetables. It makes a three-course feast. Made all over the country, the

meat content is reduced the farther from the capital you get, and every region includes its own produce. The Basques like to add red beans, and in Seville both rice and chickpeas are included, with garlic, sweet potatoes and morcilla sausage. In the south pears and pumpkins are often used, and in the Canaries, sweet potatoes and fresh corn are added.

Escudella This is the Catalan word for stew. *Escudella i carn d'olla* is a big dish, with the pork as one large dumpling, or it may contain a selection of ham, chicken, veal and sausage, with chickpeas, noodles and vegetables. *Escudella de pagès* is a

country-style stew, with carrots, potatoes and cabbage.

Fabada This is the Asturian stew of dried beans, salt pork and ham, with oak-smoked morcilla and chorizo.

Caldereta Meaning witch's cauldron, this is the name of the lamb, goat or fish stew that is cooked in it.

Estofado This is meat that is slow-cooked, usually in its fat and juice.

Guiso Also known as *guisado*, this is simply a stew with sauce.

Cochifrito Pieces of lamb or goat are fried, and seasoned with vinegar or lemon and paprika.

Fricandó Small veal pieces are stewed with vegetables.

Bread and cakes

Bread is a very important part of the Spanish diet, while cakes and sweet buns are eaten less often than in other countries. Bread shops (panaderias) sell bread alone. Cakes and other sweet things are bought from a pastelería.

BREAD

As in many European countries, *pan* is Spain's basic food and taken very seriously. Not so long ago, bread consumption was 1kg/2¼lb a head per day. In Galicia, if a piece of bread is dropped, it will be picked up and kissed. Bread also plays a ritual part in weddings, anniversaries as well as death ceremonies.

Bread accompanies all meals in Spain. It is bought twice a day and eaten very fresh. You can often see vans driving around in the mornings selling warm bread. The *barra* (long loaf) is better, some claim, than French bread. But there are a host of rolls with local names such as *bollas* (balls) and *chicas* (little girls).

Traditional breads

The wheat granary of Spain is the Tierra de Campos in León and south towards Zamora. Here they make the *hogaza* (large loaf) of Castile and the round, white *candeal* bread, which is a classic. In Catalonia, where everything tends to be done slightly differently, the bread is shaped like a three-

corned hat, with slashes across the corners. (Salvador Dalí used the hats to decorate his house.)

Pan cateto is sourdough bread with a close crumb and chewy crust (*cateto* means country bumpkin); it is dry but long lasting.

Using bread

Bread is used in a variety of ways, both in the kitchen or eaten fresh at the table.

Mojado The bread used to scoop up sauced vegetables and seafood tapas.

Rebanada A slice of bread, which is used as a "polite" plate mop at the end of a course.

Pa amb tomàquet Very lightly toasted bread, topped with olive oil and squashed fresh tomato. It is eaten at the start of every meal in parts of Catalonia. *Pan de ajo* is rubbed with a clove of garlic and drizzled with olive oil.

Torrijas These are bread dipped in milk or wine, then fried and sugared before eating.

Migas Breadcrumbs fried in olive oil and a food for all occasions, for every meal and with almost everything. They can be eaten for breakfast after a night on the town, with bacon and eggs; or with fresh fruit as dessert; they can even be eaten with chocolate and sardines – together.

Sobras Yesterday's stale bread is ideal for frying, before being pounded and used to thicken sauces and soups.

Sopa Stale pieces of bread were once breakfast fare, dunked in coffee, milk and sugar, and eaten with a spoon.

ABOVE: Pan de cebada *is a coarse-textured country bread from Galicia, which is exceptional for its barley flour.*

ABOVE: *There are numerous types of small, soft bread rolls baked in Spain. They are good at any time of day.*

ABOVE: *Small, dry* rosquillos, *made from a wine pastry, are found all over Spain.*

ABOVE: *Simple little* magdalenas (butter cakes) *make a delightful treat.*

ABOVE: Sobaos pasiegas, *from the dairy valley of Pas, are made with butter.*

BISCUITS AND COOKIES

Small dry cakes are served with sweet liqueurs, and are often dunked into them. Rings (*rosquillos*) are very common. Many little cookies are made from cinnamon pastry. Others have delightfully descriptive names. S-shaped *mostachones* look like a moustache when two of the cookies are held together; *polverones* (crumble cakes) have a powdery texture. *Macarrones* (macaroons) are made with whisked egg whites and ground almonds, while *almendrados*, made with almonds, and *almori* (honey cakes) reflect the Moorish influence. Moors' sighs (*suspiros de Moros*) are ground almond meringues.

LITTLE CAKES AND BUNS

Breakfast is the occasion for some real treats. The melting pastry of Majorcan *ensaimada*, curled like a turban, is also a favourite in Madrid. *Sobaos pasiegas* are rich butter sponges baked in little individual rectangles in papers.

Pan quemado is an all-day Valencian snack. The name means burnt bread, because it is brushed with meringue and sugar before baking, to give it a dark golden crust. For tea time in Madrid, custard-filled puff pastry *bartillos* are eaten. *Medias noches* (midnight buns) are worth sneaking down for at night.

CAKES

Sponge cakes, made with egg whites only, are light and airy and perfect for soaking up syrups and brandies – as is the tradition in Spain. *Brazo de gitano* (gypsy's arm) is the best-known cake – long and brown and rolled up round *cremadina* (custard). The big traditional cake is *Roscón de Reyes*, an enriched bread-dough ring made for Twelfth Night. It is topped with almonds and candied fruit, of which there seems to be more every year.

Spanish jam

The best jam is *cabello de angél* (angel's hair) made from the citron melon (*cidra*) which is large and blotched dark green. Jam is used to fill sweet *empanadillas* and cakes, or spread on bread.

Wine

Wine is synonymous with Spain and it accompanies practically every meal. There are two wine styles that are particular to Spain – Rioja and sherry. In Rioja, red wine (but also some white wine) is aged in oak casks, which gives it an aroma of vanilla. Sherry is a highly sophisticated fortified white wine, which in Spain is drunk as a wine, not just as an aperitif.

RED WINE

Much of Spain's wine is red, with top quality wine produced on the northern rivers and hefty reds with a high alcohol content farther south.

Wines on the Ebro river

These are the Riojas; they are soft but not delicate, with a rich fruity taste. They are blended wines, and some wine firms grow no grapes themselves. Good wines are matured partly in casks, partly in the bottle, which gives an opportunity for a "house taste".

Popular brands are San Ascensio made by Campo Viejo, the biggest *bodega* (wine firm) in Rioja, CUNE and Banda Azul (Blue Stripe) from top exporter Frederick Paternina.

Vintages are important here, as grapes may not always ripen to full potential. There are three regions of Rioja, each with its own style. Rioja Baja produces everyday fruity wines. The high Rioja Alta produces wines with more tannin, making them hard and acidic if young, but maturing to a more complex taste. By contrast, the Rioja Alavesa makes softer, aromatic wines.

Wines on the Duero river

Ribera del Duero produces Vega Sicilia, Spain's masterpiece, which is, almost unobtainable nowadays. Based on Cabernet Sauvignon, this wine is aged in casks for ten years or so. Pesquera del Duero is an alternative.

Central Spain

Valdepeñas produces better-quality. Huge *tinajas* (unglazed urns) stand at the roadsides and are used for wine. Here they make *aloques*, strong but light red wines, and *claretes*, not claret but a wine of mixed red and white grapes.

The red grapes

Tempranillo is Spain's principal red grape. Used on its own, it makes good, berry-scented young wines, but about 70 per cent of the crop goes into the great Riojas, chiefly supported by the garnacha grape.

Vast acres of Spain are under vines. La Mancha, with half the vineyards in Spain, produces red wine mainly from the *monastrell* grape. Aragón makes purplish reds, often 15 per cent by volume, because the sun raises alcohol content and diminishes quality. Cariñena, Borja, and Alicante, Jumilla and Yecla nearer the coast all make hefty reds. Priorato may be Spain's answer to Burgundy. Lighter reds come from Utiel-Requeña and Somontana.

LEFT: *Campo Viejo is one of the biggest Rioja-producing wine firms in Spain.*

The language of wine

Drinking wine is part of Spanish culture and has its own terms.

Vino de la mesa This is a house wine usually served in a pitcher.

Vino corriente This is table wine in its first or second year.

Crianza These wines must be stored for two years after harvest (*cosecha*). For the first six months the wine is stored in casks, whose oak gives the wine its distinctive flavour.

Reserva This means that the wine has been matured for three years. Both modest regional wines and good brands carry this label.

Gran reserva This includes much of the best wine, which is only made in fine vintage years or from the best grapes. Cellar-aged for six years, they have at least two years in the cask and three in the bottle.

Viña This means vineyard, but is a brand not a place. There are few estate-bottled wines.

PINK WINE

The *rosados* (rosé wines) of Navarra such as Gran Feudo are justly famous, and good ones are made in Aragón, Ribera del Duero, Tarragona and Utiel-Requeña. The cherry-coloured wines, a speciality of Ampurdán, are very good.

WHITE WINE

Good whites are produced on Spain's fringes – north and east – with the masterpiece, sherry, in the south.

Green wine

The *Alberiño* grape produces German-style wines on the slopes of Rías Bajas and Ribera del Duero. Delicately fruity, they give a slight prickle in the mouth and are perfect with shellfish.

Chacoli

The Basques are proud of this wine which they call *txacoli*. It is thin, rather acidic, with an appley flavour, and slightly sparkling.

Rioja whites

White wine is made with the traditional *viura* grape (known elsewhere as *macabeo*), usually without being aged in the cask. Marqués de Cáceres is a good example of the type. Cune's Monopole *blanco* is balanced between the two styles, while good oaked examples come from Marqués de Murrieta, Monte Real from Bodegas Riojanas and López de Heredía.

French-style whites

Lighter, fruitier and less alcoholic wines are in demand today, so styles are changing accordingly. New technology is also helping to improve white wines. Typical ones are Antonio Barbadillo in Huelva and Palacio de Bornos, made from the *verdejo* grape, in Rueda.

South-west Spain

The white wines in the south-west have a strong resemblance to sherry and include *cañamero* and *chiclana*. Most famous, however, is Montilla-Moriles, which has the same nutty scent as sherry, though it is made by conventional methods. Alvear is well-known, especially C.B. (the proprietor's initials), which is the white for cooking.

SPARKLING WINES

Cavas are wines made by the champagne method in Penedès (although the grapes may come from elsewhere), mainly in San Sadurní de Nova. Codorníu is the largest champagne-style wine producer in the world. Their top-of-the-range wine is the Chardonnay *cava*. Raimat is a good alternative, or Freixenet *cordon negro*, in the black bottle. The Spanish favour sweet *champáns* so do look for "brut" on the label.

LEFT: *Among the great sherries are Barbadillo, Tio Pepe and Domecq's La Ina.*

SHERRY

The name sherry is actually a mispronunciation of the place Jerez de la Frontera, where excellent fortified wines are produced, mainly from the *Palomino* grape, and is one of the few places in Spain with a long tradition of fine wines. Because of its high alcohol content (17 per cent by volume) and the way it is made, it is regarded as an aperitif by the outside world. But in Spain it is a white wine, the natural choice for fish, or a flamenco evening, drunk chilled from the tulip-shaped *copita*. Sherry is made in a *solera* system, a tier of barrels, where the bottom barrels are tapped and the upper barrels are made up with younger wine. The sherry is fortified with brandy, then exposed to air, where a yeast *flor* grows on the surface to protect it. Darker sherries have oxidized more.

Sherry styles

Fino This is the lightest and driest sherry. It is a pale straw colour.
Manzanilla Meaning camomile, this is similar to *fino*, but has a tang from being stored by the sea.
Amontillado This is matured until it is a soft, dark tawny colour.
Palo cortado This is sweeter still.
Oloroso With more body and a nutty flavour, *olorosos*, as a class, are on the sweet side, sometimes reminiscent of port, but they are also made in dry styles.
Cream sherry This has sweet Pedro Ximénes juice added, which gives it a voluptuous flavour.

Shopping

AUSTRALIA

Anna's Continental Fine
Foods
3/86 Scarborough Beach Road
Mount Hawthorn
Tel: (08) 9443 1508

Casa Iberica
25 Johnston Street
Fitzroy
Melbourne VIC
Tel: (03) 9419 4420

Torres Spanish Cellars
& Delicatessen
75 Liverpool Street
Sydney NSW
Tel: (02) 9264 6862

Viva Spain
315 Victoria Street
Melbourne VIC
Tel: (03) 9329 0485

NEW ZEALAND

Bel Mondo Italian
Mediterranean Foods
68 St John
St Tauranga
Tel: (07) 579 0968

Mediterranean Foods Ltd
42 Constable Street
Newtown
Wellington
Tel: (04) 939 8100

UNITED KINGDOM

Brindisa
Borough Market
London SE1
Tel: 020 7403 6932

Casa Pepe
89 High Road
London N2
Tel: 020 8444 9098

La Coruna
103 Newington Butts
London SE1
Tel: 020 7703 3165

Garcia & Sons
248–250 Portobello Road
London W11
Tel: 020 7221 6119

The Grapevine
Delicatessen
77 High Street
Odiham
Hampshire RG29
Tel: 01256 701900

Laymont & Shaw
The Old Chapel
Millpool
Truro
Cornwall TR1
Tel: 01872 270545

Lupe Pinto's Deli
24 Levan Street
Edinburgh EH3
Tel: 0131 228 6241

Maison Bouquillon
41 Moscow Road
London W2
Tel: 020 7229 2107

Moreno Wine Importers
Co Limited
11 Marylands Road
London W1
Tel: 020 7286 9678

P de la Fuente
288 Portobello Road
London W10
Tel: 020 7960 5687

Paris and Rios
93 Columbia Road
London E2
Tel: 020 7729 1147

Products from Spain
89 Charlotte Street
London W1
Tel: 020 7580 2905

Rias Altas
97 Frampton Street
London NW8
Tel: 020 7262 4340

**UNITED STATES
OF AMERICA**

Dean and Deluca
560 Broadway
New York NY 10012
Tel: (212) 226 6800

Deli Iberico
739 North LaSalle Drive
Chicago IL 60610
Tel: (312) 573 1510

New York Wine
Warehouse
8-05 43rd Avenue
Long Island City
New York NY 11101
Tel: (718) 784 8776

Michael Skurnik Wines
575 Underhill Boulevard
Suite 216
Syosset NY 11791
Tel: (516) 677 9300

The Spanish Table
1427 Western Avenue
Seattle WA 98101
Tel: (206) 682 2827

also at:
1814 San Pablo Avenue
Berkley CA 94792
Tel: (510) 548 1383

also at:
109 North Guadalupe Street
Santa Fe NM 87501
Tel: (505) 986 0243

Spectrum Ingredients
5341 Old Redwood Highway
Petaluma CA 94954
Tel: (707) 778 8900

WEBSITES
www.chefshop.com
A wide selection of mail order
Spanish ingredients and foods.

www.thecmccompany.com
A wide selection of mail order
Spanish ingredients and foods.

www.ethnicgrocer.com
A wide selection of mail order
Spanish ingredients and foods.

www.spanish-gourmet.com
Information about Spanish
ingredients and foods.

www.SpanishTaste.com
Hams, rice, and many other
Spanish foods and wines.

www.deliciosa.co.uk
Wide range of authentic
Spanish foods.

Index